A Totally Unorthodox Women's Leadership Devotional

Tiffany Tait and Lilliam Rodriguez

www.unorthodoxgroup.com

Edited by: Kelsey Knowles, MSW

Acknowledgement

As the leaders of Unorthodox Group, we differ in many ways, however we agree on one thing for sure, and that is, that God is in control. Firstly, we must acknowledge our Lord and Savior. The one who provides us with our dreams, the one who outlines our steps, and the one who covers us as we venture out into this crazy world. There has NOT been a day I can remember that HE has missed a timely word, a gentle nudge, or a firm rebuke. Every word in this planner was inspired by Him and His works in our lives. May the Lord be glorified and exalted as we lead women into the manifestation of a lifestyle designed in God's purpose and facilitated by God's gifts.

When they ask us who we are & what we do it for?

Unorthodox Group is a Strategic Business Coaching firm for faith-based women. In a nutshell, we teach other women how to hustle, develop and manifest their entrepreneurial goals while building generational wealth. We fully admit that at Unorthodox Group, we are a bit different, hence the name. We love the Lord and our spiritual relationship with God is an essential part of our story, plan, and successful financial portfolio. But so is hard work, hustle and savvy business skills. All of these factors play into our #UnorthodoxHustle. We believe in Praise, Purpose & Profits and our priorities are Faith, Family & Hustle. And that's how we live!

So... What's so Unorthodox?

At Unorthodox Group, we continually thank and praise God for the vision, favor, blessings and guidance that He has bestowed in our lives, every step of the way. But much more than that, we praise God for His patience, His imparting of long-suffering and for His denial of the multitude of our very own limiting dreams, for it is in that, we have learned true sacrifice and obedience. Those lessons have instilled in us, the long-standing values of service, humility, wisdom and success in God's Kingdom. We believe Jesus is the way, the truth and the life (John 14:6 TPT). Jesus is alive, as is the Holy Spirit that lives in us. It is in following the example of Christ (living boldly and freely in God's perfect will for our lives) and relying on the voice and direction of the Holy Spirit, that we find ourselves in line with His perfect will for our lives. The more time we spend getting to know God, honoring Him and praising Him, the clearer His will and purpose for our lives becomes. Our obedience to His spirit and His will is directly correlated with our success and fulfillment of purpose on this earth.

With that said, we are loud, flamboyant, love reggaetón and trap music. We are the daughter of immigrants and first-generation mainland Americans. We give honor to our Caribbean and Latin American roots, as well as to our ancestors and elders who have instilled the love of God in our hearts. Our success is, put simply, a result of God's grace and our #UnorthodoxHustle.

Table of Contens

Month 1

Biblical Leader: Esther
Devotion Topic: God's Expectations

[14] For if you remain silent at this time, relief and deliverance for the Jews will arise from another place, but you and your father's family will perish. And who knows but that you have come to royal position for such a time as this?

(Esther 4:14 NIV)

Esther was an orphan; her mother and father had died. Her cousin, Mordecai, took her as his own daughter and raised her. Esther was a part of the Jewish community in Persia, and as such, she had no status in society--an orphan, a woman and a minority. By all accounts, Esther was at a place of disadvantage. Despite the odds stacked against her, King Xerxes found favor in her and crowned her queen. Esther was then able to use her position to liberate the Jews in her kingdom from being destroyed and persecuted. There were, however, several steps in Esther's story that took her from the position of orphan to queen (or from a position of disadvantage to a position of advantage).

1. God gave Esther a gift: The scriptures reveal that Esther was lovely in form and features.

2. Esther prepared: She understood that despite having a natural gift from God, she would need to prepare and train in her gift. For twelve months she engaged in extensive beauty treatments at the palace, with a group of women that were all in competition to gain King Xerxes favor. Can you imagine how crazy and stressful that situation must have been? Not only did she train under those circumstances, but she also had to do it all in secrecy, to conceal her nationality.

3. Esther practiced obedience: When the king was looking for a new queen, Esther was called to the citadel of Susa, where the king was. She was obedient to Mordecai's instruction to not reveal her background and when Mordecai asked for her help the Jews, she went forward in spite of her fear.

4. Esther understood her purpose and persevered: Esther knew that she was putting herself out there and that her decision to be obedient and serve her purpose of "coming to a royal position for such a time as this" would put her life at risk. There was a strong possibility that the king could act against her for her request and secrets. Nevertheless, she moved forward to her calling.

Week 1

What are my gifts?

6 God's marvelous grace imparts to each one of us varying gifts and ministries
that are uniquely ours. So, if God has given you the grace-gift of prophecy, you
must activate your gift by using the proportion of faith you have to prophecy.
7 If your grace-gift is serving, then thrive in serving others well. If you have
the grace-gift of teaching then be actively teaching and training others.
8 If you have the grace-gift of encouragement, then use it often to encourage
others. If you have the grace gift of giving to meet the needs of others, then
may you prosper in your generosity without any fanfare. If you have the gift
of leadership, be passionate about your leadership and if you have the gift of
showing compassion, then flourish in your cheerful display of compassion.

(Romans 12:6-8 TPT)

Reflection: We are all provided with grace- gifts, things that come innate to us and that we are good at. These gifts come from God, identifying what they are, how we can develop them and how we can serve others with our God-given talents is part of God's expectations of us. God can give us any gift He desires. As unorthodox or strange as it may seem... it serves a purpose!

Action Step: What are three characteristics of yourself that you would consider to be natural gifts and/or strengths. How can these characteristics help you reach your goals?

Week 2

What does God want with me?

[37] Jesus answered him, "Love the Lord your God with every passion of your heart, with all the energy of your being, and with every thought that is within you. [38] This is the great and supreme commandment. [39] And the second is like it in importance:

'You must love your friend in the same way you love yourself.' [40] Contained within these commandments to love you will find all the meaning of the Law and the Prophets."

(Matthew 22:37-40 TPT)

Reflection: Love. God wants us to love with a full, deep agape* sort of love. He wants us to love and honor him, as well as his children. All that we do in God's Kingdom, starts with love.

Action Step: In what areas of your life do you think you can demonstrate more love?

---

*Agape (Ancient Greek ἀγάπη, agape) is a Greco-Christian term referring to unconditional love, "the highest form of love, charity" and "the love of God for man and of man for God" H. G. Liddell; Robert Scott (October 2010). An Intermediate Greek-English Lexicon: Founded Upon the Seventh Edition of Liddell and Scott's Greek-English Lexicon. Benediction Classics. p. 4. ISBN 978-1-84902-626-0.

Week 3

Why does God need me?

[14] "Your lives light up the world. Let others see your light from a distance, for how can you hide a city that stands on a hilltop? [15] And who would light a lamp and then hide it in an obscure place? Instead, it's placed where everyone in the house can benefit from its light. [16] So don't hide your light! Let it shine brightly before others, so that the commendable things you do will shine as light upon them, and then they will give their praise to your Father in heaven."

(Matthew 5:14-16 TPT)

Reflection: God needs us to keep it going. To live for Him, so others may want to live for Him. That is one of the reasons He delights in blessing us, so that others may see it and be drawn to Him.

Action Step: We often do not see ourselves as the role model God sees us as. What intentional decisions can you make to show up in this world, exactly how you would hope to?

Week 4

How do I know if my dream aligns with God's expectations of me?

[9] This is why the Scriptures say: Things never discovered or heard of before, things beyond our ability to imagine- these are the many things God has in store for all his lovers. [10] But God now unveils these profound realities to us by the Spirit. Yes, he has revealed to us his inmost heart and deepest mysteries through the Holy Spirit, who constantly explores all things.

(1 Corinthians 2:9-10 TPT)

Reflection: If we are seeking the Lord and have committed ourselves and our lives to following Him, then our dreams are given to us by Him and will always align with His expectations. They don't come from us or our desires, they come from God and are revealed to us by the Holy Spirit. According to the scripture, we don't even have the human abilities to imagine this stuff. When our dreams seem unattainable, crazy, and impossible, just know they seem that way because they didn't come from us or any other human, they came from God. They are supposed to feel out of this world, because they are!

Action Step: Have you ever felt a "tug" at your heart or a passion you just can't shake? Even if it isn't a logical or conscious desire? If so, what was that "tug"? (Hint: That's usually where our purpose starts.)

Week 5

How do I fulfill those expectations?

[23] I know, Lord, that our lives are not our own. We are not able to plan our own course. [24] So correct me, Lord, but please be gentle. Do not correct me in anger, for I would die.

(Jeremiah 10:23-24 NLT)

Reflection: Allow the above verse to be the prayer of your heart this week. May you openly allow God to direct you, guide you and gently correct you, for you are open to living in His will. You can only fulfill those expectations when you allow God to plan your course and correct you as needed.

Action Step: What are some areas of your life that you would like God to provide more clarity in? Over the next week, we challenge you to pray for God to grant you clarity in these areas. Sit patiently and allow him to show up.

Esther- God's Expectations

Wrap Up

Esther had an understanding of God's expectations of her. She took her gifts and used them for God's purpose. She could have used her beauty for many other things, yet she realized where her gift came from and that there was a purpose for that gift. God has expectations for us, expectations with the purpose of advancing His kingdom. In many cases those expectations are closely associated with our gifts. To fulfill those expectations, we must be keenly aware of what our gifts are, develop and train those gifts, practice obedience (following instruction, doing things that are scary and even going out on a limb when much is at risk) and understand how moving forward will bring us closer to our greater purpose.

Action Step: Do you believe you have a spiritual gift? If so, what is your gift? If not, what are your strengths? (Hint: Remember your natural strengths)

Action Step: Let's Brainstorm! How do you believe your gifts and/or strengths can be utilized for God's kingdom? How can they help you reach your goals?

Month 2

Biblical Leader: Deborah
Devotion Topic: Faith

"[6] She sent for Barak son of Abinoam from Kedesh in Naphtali and said to him, "The Lord, the God of Israel, commands you: 'Go take with you ten thousand men of Naphtali and Zebulun and lead the way to Mount Tabor. [7] I will lure Sisera, the commander of Jabin's army, with his chariots and his troops to the Kishon River and give him in to your hands.'" Barak said to her, "If you go with me, I will go; but if you don't go with me, I won't go." [9] "Very well," Deborah said, "I will go with you. But because of the way you are going about this, the honor will not be yours, for the Lord will hand Sisera over to a woman." So Deborah went with Barak to Kedesh"

(Judges 4:6-9 NIV)

Deborah had a strong relationship with God. God gave her the grace-gift of prophecy, and she used her faith to activate her gift. Deborah was a judge, a prophetess, and the leader of Israel. While most women were tending to their homes and families, she judged, prophesized, and went to battle. When Israelites needed help solving their disputes, they came to her. She used her gifts to help the people of Israel. In this passage, she relayed God's commandment to Barak and warned him that because he was choosing to do things on his own terms, the honor of killing Sisera would go to a woman.

He decided to follow his own plan nonetheless and Deborah joined him at the battlefield. Just as Deborah said to him, the victory of the battle went to a woman.

1.Deborah was connected to God: Deborah maintained a connection with God, she listened to God's instruction and practiced obedience.

2.Deborah activated her grace-gift: Through her faith in God, Deborah was aware of her gift and able to activate it. Because she knew God, she had faith to quick-start her gift. She believed in God and His abilities.

3.Deborah defied societal norms: Deborah was confident about what God said about her, what God had given her and what God expected of her. Despite God's expectations of her defying the status quo for women of her time, she followed Him. What others had to say, what others thought about her role and what society expected from her were non-factors, because God had spoken.

4.Deborah shattered gender roles: Deborah did not let the idea of what she or others thought was the role of women, versus the role of men, interfere with her obedience. She was not intimidated by men, instead she used the gifts that God had given her to stand up at a time when a man could not.

Week 6

How do I connect with God?

[33] So above all, constantly chase after the realm of God's kingdom and the righteousness that proceeds from him. Then all these less important things will be given to you abundantly.

(Matthew 6:33 TPT)

Reflection: The only thing that it takes for us to connect with God is to chase after him in prayer, meditation, praise and worship. There is no need to chase after anything else, because if we do this one thing the rest will be provided to us in abundance.

Action Step: Choose one activity that you can commit to for the next month, to draw closer to God. (e.g. spending an additional 15 min a day in prayer, worshipping for at least 10 min a day, reading the daily verse on an app, etc.)

Week 7

How do I increase my faith?

5 So devote yourselves to lavishly supplementing your faith with goodness,
and to goodness add understanding, 6 and to understanding add the strength
of self-control, and to self-control add patient endurance, and to patient
endurance add godliness, 7 and to godliness add mercy toward your brothers
and sisters, and to mercy toward others add unending love. 8 Since these
virtues are already planted deep within, and you possess them in abundant
supply, they will keep you from being inactive or fruitless in your pursuit of
knowing Jesus Christ more intimately.

(2 Peter 1:5-8 TPT)

Reflection: So how do we pony up? We love God. We demonstrate patience, mercy and love to those around us. And lastly, we rely on the Holy Spirit who reigns in us, to keep us motivated and dedicated to God and to our purpose.

Action Step: Increasing faith is an action item. We simply must DO IT. Faith needs to be groomed and nurtured. With that said, what is one area of your life that you have trusted God with and He successfully worked it out? (Take note of this and make it a memorial. God wants us to remember these accounts, so that we never doubt who HE is and what HE can do.)

Week 8

How do I challenge the norms of current society?

25 I give all my praises and glory to the one who has more than enough power to make you strong and keep you steadfast through the promises found in the wonderful news that I preach; that is, the proclamation of Jesus, the Anointed One.

(Romans 16:25 TPT)

Reflection: The Father, Son and Holy Spirit work in continued harmony to strengthen our spirit, increase our courage and prepare us for what is to come. Seeking God and the understanding of His will for our lives will provide us with the necessary strength to manage others' expectations of us, including managing the expectations our family and friends may have of us.

Action Step: What boundaries can you create in your personal and/or professional relationships that will allow others to set more realistic expectations of you?

Week 9

How do I SHATTER gender roles?

15 Be very careful, then, how you live- not as unwise but as wise, 16 making the
most of every opportunity, because the days are evil. 17 Therefore do not be
foolish, but understand what the Lord's will is.

(Ephesians 5:15-17 NIV)

Reflection: We shatter gender roles with wisdom. There is no need to fight, scream or prove ourselves worthy. Wisdom can be defined in many ways, however in almost all definitions of wisdom, knowledge is a part or fraction of what wisdom requires. Wisdom is not about how much we know. It includes experience, understanding, common sense, insight, and a number of other factors. Trying to shatter gender roles with knowledge instead of wisdom is next to impossible, but seeking the Lord will give us the clarity to understand when it is time to sit in silence, when it is time to speak up, when it is time to act and when it is time to let go.

Action Step: What limiting gender roles/expectations do you feel that you are held accountable to? How can you use wisdom to reformat that role, or at least the expectations of you, in that role?

Deborah- Faith

Wrap Up

Deborah was connected with God; she had a relationship with Him and knew that her abilities, strength and courage came from Him. She was able to activate her grace-gift with her faith and her faith was increased by her goodness, understanding, self-control, endurance, godliness, mercy, and unending love for others and for God. Deborah did not attempt to fit her abilities into societal norms or gender roles. Instead, she had faith in God and His purpose, enough to understand that her God-given gifts could not fit within the parameters that humans create, as we attempt to make sense of the world.

Action Step: Please list a time in your life that God has asked you for a "ridiculous" leap of faith. One in which you thought the task sounded crazy, but you knew God was asking you to do it anyway. Did you take the leap of faith? Why or why not?

Action Step: Truly reaching the heights of success that God has in store for us requires GIANT leaps of faith. Are you willing to act in faith, even before you accept your fate? (Be honest with yourself. Because this is the commitment God is looking for.) If not, that's okay! We have all been there. Now is the time to start praying for God to strengthen your faith. Just be mindful, that God will absolutely increase your faith, but He will test it first! Be prepared. Remain committed, just as Deborah did.

Month 3

Biblical Leader: Sarai, then, Sarah
Devotion Topic: Doubting God's Promises

[10] Then the Lord said, "I will surely return to you this time next year, and
Sarah your wife will have a son." Now Sarah was listening at the entrance to
the tent, which was behind him. [11] Abraham and Sarah were already old and
well advanced in years, and Sarah was past the age of childbearing. [12] Sarah
laughed to herself as she thought, "After I am worn out and my master is old,
will I now have this pleasure?"

(Genesis 18: 10-12 NLT)

Sarai was married to Abram (later Abraham), and throughout the course of their relationship, she was unable to have a child. Her husband Abram received a promise from God that he would have as many offspring as the stars in the heavens. Sarai must have been aware of what God had promised Abram, but her current state of barrenness prohibited her from feeling like a part of God's promise to her husband. Seeing Abram's disappointment at not seeing the manifestation of God's promise made Sarai feel like a roadblock to God's promise. Attempting to find a solution, she offered her maidservant (Hagar) to her husband to bear children with. This backfired when Hagar conceived. Sarai got in her feelings, mistreated the maidservant and ultimately sent her away. It was not until Sarai was confronted by the Lord for laughing and doubting God, that she became afraid. This is not explicit in the text, but her fear of the Lord must have brought her to a point of acceptance and an ultimate rendering of her control over the situation. When, and only when she finally gave up her control, God was able to show up and show out. Sarai finally understood that Abram's, now Abraham (as God had changed his name when God confirmed his covenant with him), promise was her promise. This is how Sarai became Sarah, as a confirmation from God that her husband's promise was just as much her promise.

Month 3

Biblical Leader: Sarai, then Sarah

Devotion Topic: Doubting God's Promises

1. Sarah was not aware of her promise: Sarah's challenges included not knowing HER promise. She was not aware that the promise God had given to Abram was her promise, as well.

2. Sarah thought her current state was pertinent to her promise: God didn't care that Sarah was out of childbearing age! She, on the other hand, thought her age disqualified her from the promise.

3. Sarah concocted her own plan: Sarah tried to devise her own plan to fulfill the promise and made a mess. She relied on her own understanding and ideas to attempt to fulfill a heavenly promise (unsuccessfully, of course).

4. Sarah had to give up control: Sarah attempted to control the outcome of the promise. She took over and did not have faith in God's promise. Sarah had to give up her control to see God work.

5. In spite of Sarah, God kept His promises: Sarah made a few mistakes, but God had promised to make Abram a father to many to further His kingdom. He was not going to let Sarah's doubts interfere with His plans.

Week 10

Am I hearing Him right, is He really promising me this?

[17] But the person who is joined to the Lord is one spirit with him.

(1 Corinthians 6:17 NLT))

Reflection: This simple answer is yes, if you are in communion with God (spending time in prayer and meditation) and you are obedient to His calling, He will make His desires and promises clear to you. Be mindful of the quiet whispers, gentle nudges and random coincidences that continue to show up when you ask for His guidance. It's important for us to note that His promises aren't always in line with the specific hopes and dreams that we may have had in the past. And often, we pray and do not receive an answer at all. Remember, His silence is not a dismissal, but often a reminder and sign that more time is needed in His presence.

Action Step: What are some of the things that you truly believe in your heart, will come to you, somehow, some way, in this life? (e.g., peace, wealth, health, protection) Start creating a list of all His promises, as they are revealed. Every year, reflect on this list. We are sure you will be shocked at how these promises come to fruition.

Week 11

Why Me?

[14] "For many are called, but few are chosen."

(MATTHEW 22:14 NLT)

Reflection: Where we are in life, what we have, what we don't have, what we've done or haven't done, or any other thing we may think makes HIS promise impossible, is a non-factor. Our promises are not dependent on any of those things. God has the final word and that can be whatever He says it is. God is ready to bless His kingdom, but most are not ready to show up and show out. We might feel like we're not qualified or ready, not understanding that he is not looking for our credentials, qualifications or status. He has chosen us, as we are. He simply desires a relationship with us.

Action Step: Are you ready to be chosen? We tend to believe that we are ready for the blessings God has promised us, but are you truly ready to live for God and in His perfect will? If so, jot down a simple prayer, in your own words, asking God to clearly direct your path.

Week 12

How do I know if I am doing this right?

[24] Then he said to them "Be diligent to understand the meaning behind everything you hear, for as you do, more understanding will be given to you. And according to the depth of your longing to understand, much more will be added to you. [25] For those who listen with open hearts will receive more revelation. But those who don't listen with open hearts will lose what little they think they have!"

(Mark 4:24-25 TPT)

Reflection: Don't bring in a side chick. We all question if God actually hears our prayers from time to time, but rest assured, he does. Our job is to remain patient and to continue to pray. If we are feeling lost or confused, it isn't helpful or necessary for us to intermingle our own ideas, thoughts, needs, or desires. God doesn't need our help. He will honor our longing to know Him more intimately. He will reveal His promises in time. God has a plan and as we commit ourselves and our lives to Him, He will reveal more and more to us.

Action Step: Can you identify one time in your life in which you did the opposite of what you know God was expecting of you. Ultimately, did that decision work out in a best-case scenario for you? (God wants to bless us with best-case scenarios, but those only come on His time, with His promises.)

Week 13

How do I approach God about my doubts?

15 This High Priest of ours understands our weaknesses, for he faced all of the
same testings we do, yet he did not sin. 16 So let us come boldly to the throne
of our gracious God. There we will receive his mercy, and we will find grace to
help us when we need it most.

(Hebrews 4:15-16 NLT)

Reflection: He hears us. He understands. He directs us to approach Him BOLDLY, so that is exactly what we do. We enter His presence with an open heart, an open mind, flexibility and obedience. When we try to control things that are not meant to be controlled with our own understanding, we will not get our desired outcome. We seek control because we doubt and we fear. When we let go of that doubt by keeping in constant communication with God, then our need to maintain control dissipates, because we know that all is in His hands. Simply put, we have to get out of our own way (and God's) and let Him do His thing, or we will not see the full blessing of His promise come to life.

Action Step: Guilt, shame, church-hurt, fear of judgment... are all reasons we shun areas of our life from God. But he wants us to be open and honest about our fears and doubts. What are you afraid to go to God about? Boldly, write out your thoughts, fears and doubts. Now lay them at the altar, give them to God and keep hustling!

Week 14

What are His plans?

29 For God's gifts and his call can never be withdrawn.

(Romans 11:29 NLT)

Reflection: God has an ultimate plan, that plan is to further His kingdom. He provides us with spiritual gifts and promises as He calls us into certain positions, in order for us to further His kingdom. No matter how much we mess up, God will NOT withdraw His gifts and call. It is important to note that we can delay and prohibit the manifestations of His promises and calling, with our own disobedience. However, when we decide to seek the

Lord, we can always return to our calling. It is also important to acknowledge that our disobedience has consequences and those consequences can include us running out of time (even death), in which case, we will not see the manifestations of His promises. However, while there is time and life, our gifts and calling are present, manifested, or on standby.

Action Step: As a starting place on a journey to living in purpose, how do you see yourself being able to play a role in God's larger plan for His Kingdom? (e.g. volunteering, teaching, donating, coaching, praying, healing, etc.) Please be specific.

Sarai, then Sarah- Doubting God's Promises

Wrap Up

Sarah had to learn her promise, she had to realize that her age and her history had nothing to do with her promise. She had to come to terms with the fact that God would uphold His promise, despite her doubt. She had to fail at her own plans with Hagar, to learn to give up control. God has a promise for you. And like Sarah, you have to know what that promise is and accept that your current state does not qualify or disqualify you. It is not your job to come up with a strategy to inherit this promise, you simply have to turn over control to God. You can align yourself with Him, be a part of His plan and see His promises fulfilled or you can choose to NOT be a part of it. Just know that His ultimate plan will move forward, with or without you.

Have you ever felt the regret of distrusting a promise that someone has made to you, and then they actually come through? Imagine how Sarah must have felt. Below, make a list of the areas of your life where you are willing to relinquish doubt and fight fear, because you KNOW God is in control. (Add this list to your daily prayer. Ask God to allow you to remove any doubts you may have in these areas of your life.)

Month 4

Biblical Leader: Ruth
Devotion Topic: Commitment

"[15] "Look," said Naomi, "your sister-in-law is going back to her people and her gods. Go back with her." [16] But Ruth replied "Don't urge me to leave you or to turn back from you. Where you go I will go, and where you stay I will stay. Your people will be my people and your God my God." [17] Where you die I will die, and there I will be buried. May the Lord deal with me, be it ever so severely, if anything but death separates you and me. [18] When Naomi realized that Ruth was determined to go with her, she stopped urging her.

(Ruth 1:15-18)

Ruth was from Moab and was married to Mahlon. Mahlon had immigrated to Moab from Judah with his parents, Naomi and Elimelech, and his brother. His brother married Orpah, another Moabitess. When his father, Elimelech, died, his mother Naomi became a widow. Mahlon and his brother later died, widowing Ruth and Orpah. Naomi decided to return to Judah and urged Ruth and Orpah to return to their families. Orpah returned home, but Ruth insisted on going with Naomi. Ruth promised Naomi, she would accompany her on the journey to Bethlehem (Naomi's home). They arrived just in time for the barley harvest. Ruth offered to go pick up leftover grain behind the harvesters and ended up in a field that belonged to Boaz, a relative of Naomi's with good standing. Boaz was in the area and asked the foreman about Ruth. The foreman explained that Ruth was the Moabitess who traveled with Naomi. Boaz offered Ruth food, shelter, and protection. Ruth questioned why he found favor in her and Boaz replied that he had heard about all that she had done for her mother-in-law. Naomi then spoke with Ruth about finding a new husband and gave Ruth specific instructions to follow with Boaz. Ruth followed Naomi's instruction and Boaz promised to help her. He later married Ruth and they bore a son named Obed. Obed became the grandfather of King David, making Ruth part of the lineage of Jesus.

Month 4

Biblical Leader: Ruth
Devotion Topic: Commitment

1. Ruth's loss: Ruth left her home to marry, lost her husband, and was forced to forfeit her land. She must have been filled with disappointment and despair. She then moved to Bethlehem with Naomi who was likely experiencing difficulties and resentments from her own losses. A history of religious and political conflicts led to a tense relationship between the Israelites and the people of Moab, so Ruth had to contend with this bitterness in addition to her grief. With the loss of their husbands, Naomi and Ruth also lost their financial stability and the vision they had for their futures. In the face of all these challenges, Ruth was firm in her commitment to Naomi. One can imagine it was not easy for Ruth to support Naomi given the known conflict between the Israelite and Moabite people.

2. Ruth's righteousness: Despite her losses, Ruth practiced righteousness. She remained with her mother-in-law, who was now older, alone, unable to work or sustain herself, and about to embark on a journey back to her homeland. Naomi was probably not the nicest person to be around, given the circumstances, however, Ruth understood that Naomi needed her and she needed Naomi and Naomi's God. Ruth proceeded with her commitment.

3. Ruth is humble: Ruth practiced humility in order to fulfill her commitment. Ruth was humble when Naomi insisted and pushed her to go home. Ruth was humble when she chose to travel to Bethlehem despite the rejection she might face. Ruth was humble when she offered to pick-up leftover grain, the scraps others left behind. At any point Ruth could have said 'I will take care of things on my own', or 'I am grieving too'. This reaction would've been understandable considering her personal losses. But instead, she practiced humility and obedience. All to uphold her promise and commitment

4. Ruth chose her network wisely: Ruth could have gone back home, but I am sure that back home with her native gods, she did not experience the God she had seen in Naomi and the family she married into. Ruth not only promised to stay with Naomi, but she also seemed to understand that she needed Naomi if she was to leave her home. If Ruth was embarking on this journey, she needed support and Naomi could offer her guidance, even if Naomi was working through her own difficulties.

Week 15

How do I endure loss?

[20] Now may the God of peace— who brought up from the dead our Lord Jesus, the great Shepherd of the sheep, and ratified an eternal covenant with his blood— [21] may he equip you with all you need for doing his will. May he produce in you, through the power of Jesus Christ, every good thing that is pleasing to him. All glory to him forever and ever! Amen.

(Hebrews 13: 20-21 NLT)

Reflection: Ruth's loss propelled her to her next level. When we experience a loss, in particular the loss of a loved one, it can look and feel, like the end of us. Even when it feels like we have lost everything, God will ensure that we have all that we need to endure. He will build and create things in us and around us. Things we have never imagined. Don't worry about how to endure. That's HIS job. He ensures that we endure. Our job is to keep our commitment to God.

Action Step: What is a loss that you have experienced in your life? Has this loss stagnated or hindered your relationship with God? Dig DEEP: How can you use this deep loss to propel you further into your purpose in God's Kingdom?

Week 16

How do I do the right thing?

[8] For athletic training only benefits you for a short season, but righteousness brings lasting benefit in everything; for righteousness contains the promise of life, for time and eternity.

(1 Timothy 4:8 TPT)

Reflection: God wants us to train with Him. Training means spending quality time with God through prayer and meditation. When we pray, we ask God the questions in our hearts, and when we meditate, we sit in silence, enjoy his presence and listen for His answer. Through our ongoing communication with God, He will develop in us our trust, faith, integrity and obedience. This training builds our relationship with God, provides us with a clear path to act and live-in righteousness and holds us accountable for successfully maintaining our commitments.

Action Step: What two things can you do this week to start (or increase) your training schedule with God? (e.g., reading my bible nightly, praying with a friend once a week, etc.)

Week 17

Humility what?!?

12 For whoever exalts himself will be humbled, and whoever humbles himself will be exalted.

(Matthew 23:12 NIV)

Reflection: God is preparing us for great things, but that road requires humility. It requires humility to understand the perspective of others and to hold a high position. If we seek humility in all we do, God will take care of us. If we choose to exalt ourselves, we will face humiliation. Without humility it will be hard to maintain focus on our commitment.

Action Step: Being humble doesn't mean lacking success. It simply means knowing who to give the credit to. So, let's talk about all the success we've had as a result of God's grace and our hustle. Please begin your "Testimony Receipt List" below. Write out and acknowledge all the times God has shown up for you in your life. (i.e., continuous reminders of this list are exactly what we need to remain focused and encouraged)

Week 18

Who is my network?

[11] So encourage each other and build each other up, just as you are already doing.

(1 Thessalonians 5:11 NLT)

Reflection: We must be mindful of the people we choose to associate, congregate, fellowship, take trips with... you all get it! Be mindful of who your friends and confidants are. As you continue to grow and excel, those in your circle will either build you or break you down. They will literally place themselves in one basket or the other. Be mindful of how you fill your baskets.

Action Step: Who's in your corner? List any friends, business associates, family members, etc. that you consider to be part of your inner circle. (Really take a moment to slow down and think about this one. Review this list over time and adjust as necessary. As you grow, your priorities will change. This is healthy and normal, but that isn't necessarily the case for those around you. Protect your peace.)

Ruth- Commitment

Wrap Up

Ruth experienced the loss of her husband, yet she proceeded forward. She understood the importance of practicing righteousness, and she did what was right by her mother-in-law despite the hardships she might face. She was humble when she needed to be, and these actions directly lead her to a secure future with Boaz, impacting generations to come. Ruth knew who her support network was. She knew that Naomi served a powerful God and that Naomi had knowledge and understanding that she did not have. Ruth stuck with her and relied on her for direction, not because of who Naomi was, but because of her commitment.

God wants us to understand that there will be loss in this journey, despite that, He provides us with tools to endure those losses. Righteousness is essential to dealing with loss, it is a moral compass to pursue. Even when life looks completely crazy around us, when we're desperate beyond belief, when we have nothing left to give spiritually, physically, or financially; righteousness is still expected. Not having, lacking and experiencing loss is not a green light to act out and demand our own way. Instead, we must continue to seek God's righteousness and continue to do the next right thing. During times of loss, humility is a must. Humility reminds us that God's ways are higher than our own. His understanding is higher than our understanding and despite what our eyes are seeing right now, God has this covered.

God will strategically place others in our path who can provide us with the exact support or resources we require in a time of need. We must be mindful of who those individuals are. Be on the lookout. Pray for discernment. Choose wisely, identify those that have God in their hearts and can provide you with wise instruction.

Action Step: What commitments have you followed through in your life, despite not desiring to do so? Often, God will require us to make and follow through with commitments that are not our own desires, but necessary to fulfill His purpose and promise in our lives. The examples you list below are simply training exercises for the bigger promise. God will test our commitment, patience, and resilience. Hold strong. God is good and He sees your sacrifices.

Action Step: What spiritual role models or support systems do you have in your personal life? Are you fully utilizing the benefit of this support system? (If you do not have a support system in this area, we strongly encourage you to reach out to a small, local group, at a church of your choosing.)

Month 5

Biblical Leader: Bathsheba
Devotion Topic: YOUR Story

2 One evening David got up from his bed and walked around on the roof of the
palace. From the roof he saw a woman bathing. The woman was very beautiful,
3 and David sent someone to find out about her. The man said, "Isn't this
Bathsheba, the daughter of Eliam and the wife of Uriah the Hittite?" 4 Then
David sent messengers to get her. She came to him and he slept with her.
Then she went back home. 5 The woman conceived and sent word to David,
saying, "I am pregnant."

(2 Samuel 1:2-5)

Bathsheba was married to Uriah. Uriah was away fighting a war. One day she was bathing herself and King David saw her and was attracted to her beauty. He inquired about her and discovered she was married. But he still summoned her and slept with her. Bathsheba conceived and sent word to the king. The king brought Uriah back from the war and told him to go home, however Uriah refused. When the king asked why, Uriah told him he cannot go home while his men are still out fighting. The king then invited Uriah to eat and drink until Uriah was drunk, but Uriah still did not go home. The king sent Uriah back to the war zone with a note for Joab, the leader of the army. The letter instructed Joab to place Uriah at the front of the confrontation so he would be killed. Joab did as he was instructed and just as the king had planned, Uriah was killed. Bathsheba mourned the loss of her husband, but after she was done mourning, the king summoned her again, married her and she bore him a son. King David's actions displeased the Lord. As a consequence of his sin, his son with Bathsheba dies. King David proceeded to console his wife and they conceived another son, Solomon. Solomon was loved by the Lord, making Bathsheba the mother of the wisest and richest man on earth. Bathsheba's situation was problematic to say the least, however in spite of what was done to her, God rewarded her throughout her life. The son she bore for David, Solomon, rose up to bless her in mighty ways. God blessed her in spite of her circumstances.

1. The Setting: Bathsheba is the main character of this story; she is said to be beautiful and the wife of Uriah. Bathsheba lives in Jerusalem at the time when King David reigns over Jerusalem. This was a time when women were under the tutelage of men and men ruled over women. A time when Bathsheba would have had little to no control over her life or her own body.

2. The Plot: Bathsheba is summoned by the king, the most powerful man in all Jerusalem. At his command, she went to see the King. While she was there, he slept with her. It is not described in the bible whether this act was rape or consensual but we do know that there was definitely inequality between King David and Bathsheba, at minimum.

3. The Conflict: Bathsheba then conceives and tells David. David attempts to hide his sin and kills Bathsheba's husband. Bathsheba mourns his loss and then faces tragedy again after the loss of the baby she conceived with David, all due to the sins of a man.

4. The Resolution: But God!!! The resolution, our Redeemer! He has a purpose higher than any man, any woman, any sin. He allows Bathsheba to conceive a son named Solomon. Solomon, who would later become King of Israel, the wisest and wealthiest man in the world, a man who honors his mother even when he sits on a royal throne. Bathsheba, out of an act of sin against her, gives birth to God's purpose.

Week 19

Your Setting:

28 And we know that in all things God works for the good of those who love him, who have been called according to his purpose.

(Romans 8:28 NIV)

Reflection: Our setting, where we are from, the societal stipulations of our time, politics, discrimination, marginalization, none of these things can take away our calling to His purpose. Our setting does not define our purpose. As a matter of fact, it is often the setup for our purpose.

Action Step: What was your "setting"? What is something about YOU that the devil would love to use for his misery, but that you are determined to use for God's glory?

Week 20

Your Plot:

46 Mary responded, "Oh, how my soul praises the Lord. 47 How my spirit rejoices
in God my Savior! 48 For he took notice of his lowly servant girl, and from now
on all generations will call me blessed.

(Luke 1:46-48 NLT)

Reflection: How our story starts will not be how our story ends. Our story might be filled with twists and turns. There might be loss, trauma, pain, shame, scarcity, things others have done against us, etc. but God is still saying to us, "generations will call you blessed".

Action Step: The bible says, "generations will call you blessed". This is HIS promise! But it cannot be revealed to us until we truly accept and believe in our hearts that God wants more for us and is ready to bless us. Use the space below to ask God to bless your ending. Let God know the desires of your heart and your commitment to His will. And now, walk in faith.

Week 21

Your Conflict:

[1] What causes fights and quarrels among you? Don't they come from your desires that battle within you? [2] You want something but don't get it. You kill and covet but cannot have what you want. You quarrel and fight. You do not have, because you do not ask God. [3] When you ask, you do not receive, because you ask with wrong motives, that you may spend what you get on your pleasures.

(James 4:1-3)

Reflection: The desires, sin and disobedience of others can and will mark our lives, as it did Bathsheba's. Yet, this is not an excuse to pursue our own desires. God instructs us to just ask Him for what we want with the correct intentions. What are the correct intentions? They are not intentions to enrich ourselves, but intentions to further His Kingdom.

Action Step: How do your desires for your life align with a greater purpose to further God's kingdom? For instance, do you believe your goals fill the purpose God has for you here on earth? (If there is no alignment, begin to pray that God reveals His purpose for you. Be open to His will, not just your desires.)

Week 22

Your Resolution:

[9] Their descendants will be recognized and honored among the nations. Everyone will realize that they are a people the Lord has blessed.

(Isaiah 61:9 NLT)

Reflection: God continues to remind us that we will be set apart, not set aside. He promises us that we will be recognized, honored and blessed for our obedience and willingness to use our lives, our gifts and our stories to lead others.

Action Step: Understanding it is our joy and honor to give God the glory in ALL things, what is YOUR desired legacy? How do you want to be remembered when it is all said and done?

Bathsheba- YOUR Story

Wrap Up

Bathsheba did not have much control over her life. The setting of her time left her at the will of men. The sins of King David involve her and eventually pull her into a story of pain and loss. Yet the trespasses of others, the control of others and her continued losses lead her to a place of purpose. The times we live in, what others have done against us, how other people have involved us in their mess and the grief we are experiencing, is the core of our purpose. It is not God's desire to have us undergo all this pain and suffering. However, because of the sin of others and even our own sin, experiencing suffering is a part of the story. Let it be clear that pain and suffering are NOT the end of us. Our loss is not our end. Our TRAUMA is not our end. If we hand those over to God, that pain, that loss, that traumatic experience will become a part of our purpose in God's plan. And will be only the beginning.

Action Step: If we allow ourselves to heal from all of our hurt and pain, no matter how deep the wound is, that healing can become the birthplace of our purpose and our ministries. What are you willing to allow yourself to heal from, so that you can live in your purpose?

Action Step: Depending on whose version you read, Bathsheba can be cast as dishonest, strategic, dependent, traumatized, an adulteress... Ultimately, none of these opinions had any impact on her purpose. What self-prescribed or given labels are you willing to let go of right now? List them below and let them go! They will not determine your purpose, nor will they impact your promise ever again!

Month 6

Biblical Leader: Hannah
Devotion Topic: Obedience

10 In bitterness of soul Hannah wept much and prayed to the Lord. 11 And she made a vow, saying, “O Lord Almighty, if you will only look upon on your servant’s misery and remember me, and not forget your servant but give her a son, then I will give him to the Lord for all the days of his life, and no razor will ever be used on his head.”... 24 After he was weaned, she took the boy with her, young as he was, along with a three-year-old bull, an ephah of flour and a skin of wine, and brought him to the house of the Lord at Shiloh 25 When they had slaughtered the bull, they brought the boy to Eli, 26 and she said to him, “As surely as you live, my lord, I am the woman who stood here beside you praying to the Lord. 27 I prayed for this child, and the Lord has granted me what I asked of Him. 28 So now I give him to the Lord. For his whole life he will be given over to the Lord. And he worshiped the Lord there.

(1 Samuel 1:10-11, 24-28 NIV)

Hannah was a barren woman; she had not given birth to any children. In those times, not grossly unlike the present, children were considered blessings. Any woman who did not bear children would be considered cursed. To make matters worse for Hannah, her husband had two wives (as was the custom of the time). The other wife, Peninnah, bore Hannah’s husband many children.

Peninnah provoked Hannah to the point that Hannah wept and would not eat. But the scriptures state that because Hannah's husband loved her, he would give a portion of the meat to Peninnah and their children, but to Hannah he gave a double portion. Hannah wanted children so badly, she often cried and prayed. One day, while she was praying in the house of the Lord, she vowed to God that if He would give her a son, she would give her son to the Lord for all the days of his life. The priest, Eli, saw Hannah's mouth moving but heard no words coming out. Eli thought that Hannah was drunk and confronted her. Hannah responded, no, "I am a woman who is deeply troubled... and am praying out of my anguish and grief". Eli sent her off in peace. After her prayer, Hannah conceived a son and named him Samuel meaning "because I asked the Lord for him". When it was time to go offer the annual sacrifice to the Lord, Hannah did not go with her husband. Instead, she explained that she would finish weaning the child and then take him and present him before the Lord to live there always. The intention was for the child to stay at the temple in the care of the high priest, Eli. Hannah's husband replied, "Do what seems best to you". When Samuel was weaned, but still a toddler, she took him to the house of the Lord in Shiloh and gave him over. Hannah was then blessed with many other children.

Month 6

Biblical Leader: Hannah
Devotion Topic: Obedience

1. Hannah was barren: Hannah must have felt mortified, annoyed, disgusted and isolated. She must have been experiencing conflicting emotions and thoughts about herself and her situation. Not only was she lacking something she considered important, but something that others, maybe even her husband, deemed vital. She was ridiculed arguably to the point of being bullied by the other wife, year after year. Her self-esteem crumbled. The bible states she was deeply troubled, cried often and did not eat; all symptoms of what we now know as depression. She was depressed and hopeless about her barrenness.

2. Hannah's prayer: There was nothing anyone could do for Hannah. There was nothing she could do to change her state of barrenness. But she knew God could turn her situation around. She went on her knees and prayed from her heart, so frenzied that the priest thought she was drunk. She laid it all out for God, right there in the temple. She laid down her barrenness, her pain, her shame, her depression and brokenness. She surrendered at God's altar in her state of desperation, even at the cost of looking crazy.

3. Hannah was loved: The scripture states that Hannah's husband LOVED her. He saw her pain and did what he could to support her. When Hannah made her vow to God to give up her son, he stepped out of her way and said,

"Do what seems best to you". His love covered her and supported her to such a degree that he was willing to give up his son (the son he conceived with the woman he loved, the son he knew his wife longed for and suffered for) without so much as a word of hesitation. Only his love for Hannah could have allowed him that level of unconditional support and understanding.

4. Hannah was obedient: When Hannah initially made her vow to God she was in a deep depression: troubled, crazed, and desperate. It would have been easy to say anything, even to God, to get what she wanted. When she held her baby in her hands, nursed him and took care of him; the feelings she experienced must have been beyond bliss. She was in an entirely different emotional state from when she made her plea and promise. Experiencing what it felt like to hold her baby close to her and look down at the one thing she had longed for, while also knowing that she made a vow to give all that up, could have really backfired for Hannah. She could have ignored her promise, asked for a second chance, or explained away her crazy promise due to her mental state. But Hannah chose obedience. Hannah chose to follow through. Hannah chose to honor God and present her only child to Him.

Week 23

Our Barrenness:

25 "Therefore I tell you, do not worry about your life, what you will eat or drink;
or about your body, what you will wear. Is not life more than food, and the
body more than clothes? 26 Look at the birds of the air; they do not sow or
reap or store away in barns, and yet your heavenly Father feeds them. Are
you not much more valuable than they? 27 Can any one of you by worrying add
a single hour to your life? 28 "And why do you worry about clothes? See how
the flowers of the field grow. They do not labor or spin. 29 Yet I tell you that
not even Solomon in all his splendor was dressed like one of these. 30 If that
is how God clothes the grass of the field, which is here today and tomorrow
is thrown into the fire, will he not much more clothe you —you of little faith?

(Matthew 6:25-30 NIV)

Reflection: The barrenness we are experiencing might not be literal, in the sense that we are unable to bear children. Our barrenness could be anything that we are unable to produce by ourselves. We could be financially barren, spiritually barren, psychologically barren, physically barren, emotionally barren, etc. We all have something we lack or can't do for ourselves. We could feel like a bawse, build empires as an entrepreneur, bank billions, obtain more power than we would know what to do with and still question our worth in this world. As humans, we are often prone to searching for love and/or acceptance in all the wrong places. Financial stability obviously allows us access to more tangible means, but it does NOT put us in a position where we are utterly self-sufficient. We all experience barrenness, but God promises He is all we need, no matter the circumstance.

Action Step: Do you ever doubt yourself, question your worth or wonder if you are simply good enough? Welp, if so, you are in good company. We've all been there. What is an area of your life that you doubt your skills or ability to achieve success? What is your barrier to achieving success in this area?

Week 24

How should I pray?

[6] Do not be anxious about anything, but in every situation, by prayer and petition, with thanksgiving, present your requests to God.

(Philippians 4:6 NIV)

Reflection: We can pray on our knees, standing, while driving, in our hearts, in bed, alone, with company, by talking to ourselves, while working-out or cooking, in our heads, or on our bathroom break (we all know about texting and talking while running to the restroom). The bible literally says, "in every situation" and that means ANY situation we might find ourselves in. The way we call to the Lord is going to depend on what the situation is and how we feel about it. When we are going to ask the boss for a promotion, we come prepared and with reverence. When we are spilling the tea to our home girl (hopefully spiritual tea), we are detailed and intrigued. When we get a promotion and get home, we scream and jump. When we are happy and celebrating, we sing and dance. We come to God in prayer as we are, where we are and how we feel.

Action Step: This week, we would like you to practice what we call "spot prayers". Throughout the day, pick at least 3x to quickly say a prayer in your head. (one prayer of gratitude, one prayer for peace, one prayer for clarity). Continue this every day for 1 week. This is an exercise to get us in the habit of going to God, first. With every thought, every emotion, every desire, we need to train ourselves to go to God in prayer, first.

Week 25

What Love?

[4] Rise up; this matter is in your hands. We will support you, so take courage and do it."

(Ezra 10:4 NIV)

Reflection: At this point we might be asking ourselves, 'who loves me like Hannah's husband loved her?' Or we may already know who loves us. This is not necessarily love from a partner. It might be the love of a child, the love of a parent, the love of a friend; anyone who sees our barrenness and loves us despite it. This is a person who is directly impacted by our obedience to God, impacted by our calling and is on this journey with us voluntarily or involuntarily. This is a person who sees or doesn't see the measures we are willing to take to follow God's purpose and still says, "Do what seems best to you". We must embrace those people in our lives. We must acknowledge them and honor them. Because if we think the ride of our lives is crazy, imagine how they must be feeling while they ride with us, in the passenger seat. They didn't ask for this, but because they love us, they step to the side so we can follow God's dream.

Action Step: List the people who have been in your corner and "held you down" along the way. We need to make a conscious effort to acknowledge the people that God has placed in our lives, that continue to support us, love us, and guide us. We challenge you to say a quick thank you to each person on your list.

Week 26

What does obedience mean for me?

1 "If you fully obey the Lord your God and carefully keep all His commands
that I am giving you today, the Lord your God will set you high above all the
nations of the world. 2 You will experience all these blessings if you obey the
Lord your God: 3 Your towns and your fields will be blessed. 4 Your children
and your crops will be blessed. The offspring of your herds and flocks will be
blessed. 5 Your fruit baskets and breadboards will be blessed. 6 Wherever you
go and whatever you do, you will be blessed. (Deuteronomy 28:1-6 NLT)

Reflection: The bible is very clear. If we obey God's direction in our lives, we will be blessed. But let's be clear. Our unimaginable and miraculous blessings are contingency-based. Our inheritance of those blessings is directly correlated to our obedience to His will.

Action Step: What has God asked of you in your life? Have you shown obedience to God's requests and direction for your life or disobedience? Remember, just because we demonstrate obedience doesn't mean our circumstances will change overnight. But if we continue in disobedience, we can rest assured we risk never seeing His promises fulfilled in our lives.

Hannah- Obedience

Wrap Up

Hannah was barren and could not conceive a child. She suffered and was troubled by this. By today's standards, she might have been considered depressed. Hannah knew that God was the only one who could do for her. She asked God for her gift and committed her unborn child to the Lord. The Lord conceded her the desire of her heart and Hannah bore a son. Now Hannah had to bring the child to the Lord. Hannah's husband, out of the love he felt for her and having witnessed her long-suffering, understood this was something Hannah had to do. He stepped aside and Hannah obediently presented the child to the Lord. Out of our barrenness and lack will grow a desire that can only be settled with God's divine intervention. This divine intervention can only be provoked by prayer and this prayer can only be manifested through obedience. In all this, we must be mindful of those around us who are impacted by our barrenness and obedience. We must be grateful for those relationships and consider ourselves privileged to have their love.

Action Step: We focused a lot on how other people impact our lives, but more importantly, how are we impacting others? Describe, in detail, how you are showing up in this world, right now. Are you a positive, negative or neutralizing force for those around you?

Action Step: How does my obedience (or disobedience) impact those around me?

Month 7

Biblical Leader: Abigail
Devotion Topic: Success

24 She fell at his feet and said: "My lord, let the blame be on me alone. Please
let your servant speak to you; hear what your servant has to say. 25 May my
lord pay no attention to that wicked man Nabal. He is just like his name - his
name is Fool, and folly goes with him. But as for me, you servant, I did not
see the men my master sent. 26 "Now since the Lord has kept you, my master,
from bloodshed and from avenging yourself with your own hands, as surely
as the Lord lives and as you live, may your enemies and all who intend to
harm my master be like Nabal. 27 And let this gift, which your servant has
brought to my master, be given to the men who follow you. 28 Please forgive
your servant's offense, for the Lord will certainly make a lasting dynasty for
my master, because he fights the Lords' battles. Let no wrongdoing be found
in you as long as you live.

(1 Samuel 25:24-28 NIV)

Abigail was married to a wealthy man named Nabal. They lived in Moab, a desert, which also happened to be the place where David was on the run from Saul. The scriptures tell us that Abigail was an intelligent and beautiful woman, but her husband was surly and mean in his dealings. David heard that Nabal was sheep-shearing (or preparing for festivities), so he sent men to remind Nabal of how he protected his shepherds in the past and to ask for whatever Nabal could give him and his men. Nabal responded that he did not know David, a rejection of his plea for help. When David got word of Nabal's insult he was furious and asked his men to grab their swords and head toward Nabal. One of the servants ran ahead to give Abigail the heads up, so that she was prepared. The servant revealed that David sent his men to greet Nabal and Nabal insulted them, even though David and his men had protected Nabal's household and belongings. The servant urged Abigail to do something, as disaster was looming over Nabal and their home. Abigail, a savvy wife, started hustling immediately. She loaded food onto the donkeys and sent her servants to David to present the goods to him and his men. She then traveled separately to meet David, without telling her husband of her plans. Meanwhile, David decided to take matters into his own hands and handle the situation (Nabal) himself. On his way, David ran into Abigail on the road.

She pleaded with him to blame her alone, to pay no attention to foolish Nabal and to please accept her gifts. She asked for forgiveness, reminded David of God's promises to him and urged David to let God handle Nabal. David blessed her for her good judgement in keeping him from the bloodshed he was about to incur. He accepted her request. When Abigail returned home, Nabal was drunk. She waited until the morning, when he was sober, to tell him what had transpired. His heart failed him and ten days later he died. David asked her to marry him and Abigail became known as one of the few female prophetesses of her time.

Month 7

Biblical Leader: Abigail
Devotion Topic: Success

1. Abigail's "success": In the eyes of many, Abigail already fit the definition of success; wealthy, beautiful, intelligent, and well-connected. But God had another take on success for Abigail. His definition of success, I'm sure, differed from Abigail's. However, Abigail stayed open and flexible to God's will, which ultimately led to her ultimate success.

2. Abigail took the challenge: When the servant warned Abigail of what had happened and the possible outcome, Abigail intercepted and interceded (literally and spiritually). She could have chosen to stay in a "woman's place", which would have been the custom of her day, but instead she rose to the occasion and accepted the challenge. She took responsibility for it all. Abigail knew when to speak up and what to say. Abigail firmly understood that her humility was also her strength.

3. Abigail took perspective: When things went awry due to her husband's poor judgment, Abigail adjusted her perspective. She came before David, her face on the ground (literally). At that moment, she must have felt anxious, unsure of her future, scared and alone in the hands of powerful enemies. Abigail was on her own and had no physical army to protect her. But Abigail didn't let any of those barriers interfere in her success. She understood her priorities and her responsibilities and didn't allow any internal emotion to sway her decisions.

4. Abigail knew the Lord: Abigail walked around knowing what she was working with. She knew the shortcomings on her side (her husband's ways). She knew of God's promises (she was aware of what was going on spiritually at the time and the promises God had made David). She also knew about the Lord's ways (she tells David to avoid wrongdoings). But knowing all those things simply isn't enough. It was Abigail's faith, quick thinking and savvy that saved her family from destruction. The ability to demonstrate such wisdom was the product of Abigail's own connection with God.

Week 27

Success: Our definition vs. God's definition:

[3] Before you do anything, put your trust totally in God and not in yourself. Then every plan you make will succeed.

(Proverbs 16:3 TPT)

Reflection: Abigail was successful by most people's definition, but God had another idea. Our definition of success and God's definition of success can sometimes align, but our methods often differ. Saving her home, becoming a part of history and a powerful prophetess was God's intention. Sure, beauty and intelligence are good things to have, but what God had in mind surpassed that. The bible is very clear on this topic: set your goals, but commit yourself fully to God's method of execution, His timing and His periodic adjustments. Ultimately, trust and follow Him and you will succeed.

Action Step: In what area(s) are you not FULLY trusting God right now because the promise is taking much longer to arrive than expected? (Include this area in your daily prayers and ask God to bless you with patience as you wait on his perfect timing.)

Week 28

Accepting the challenge of success:

[3] Be free from pride-filled opinions, for they will only harm your cherished unity. Don't allow self-promotion to hide in your hearts, but in authentic humility put others first and view others as more important than yourselves.

(Philippians 2:3 TPT)

Reflection: We must start from a place of humility and willingness to follow God's will. From there we can set goals based on our righteous motives and perspectives. Accepting the challenges of being a successful woman/man of God will require humility. Had Abigail thought highly of herself for her current success, she would not have been in a position to accept the challenge that ultimately led to her most notable success.

Action Step: We often don't maximize our own potential due to our personal fears of failure. But our fears are based on our perceptions. Our perceptions are developed either through our lens of trauma or our lens of healing (if we've healed). Our perspective on challenges and our role in those predicaments, needs to remain open and flexible, as did Abigail's. What areas do you lack flexibility that God may be trying to work with you on?

Week 29

Success is about perspective:

9 So I became greater than all who had lived in Jerusalem before me, and my
wisdom never failed me. 10 Anything I wanted; I would take. I denied myself no
pleasure. I even found great pleasure in hard work, a reward for all my labors.
11 But as I looked at everything, I had worked so hard to accomplish, it was all
so meaningless—like chasing the wind. There was nothing really worthwhile
anywhere.

(Ecclesiastes 2:9-11 NLT)

Reflection: What do you consider success? Does that perspective serve God's perfect will? Will that view of success be worth it? We must be mindful of our preconceived ideologies regarding success and the perspective from which we view success. We can view success in such a way that sometimes we achieve it and realize that it was not all it seemed cracked up to be. Maintaining perspective about our purpose, alignment with God, dedication to His calling and a wide-angle view of our hustle becomes even more important when we are defining our accomplishments and success as it pertains to God.

Action Step: How will you KNOW when you're successful? What will that look like? (i.e., I will know I'M successful because I will have a fulltime job as a manager, my children will be doing well in school and I will have a substantial savings account.) Bookmark this page. It may be a part of your testimony one day. But don't worry if it's not. God's goals and His ultimate blessings for us, are usually unimaginable.

Week 30

Living with Success according to God

[48] But someone who does not know, and then does something wrong, will be punished only lightly. When someone has been given much, much will be required in return; and when someone has been entrusted with much, even more will be required.

(Luke 12:48 NLT)

Reflection: A certain level of connection, relationship, or intimacy with the Lord is a prerequisite for achieving success according to God's will. Without this connection, success in His Kingdom, is unlikely. It is key for that connection with God to exist. Firstly, this connection will equip you and secondly it will help you manage the load and burden of success. In other words, "To whom much is given, much is required". Know that the Lord will bless us in unimaginable fashion, but we will be held accountable every step of the way. His standards are high, but His rewards are GREAT.

Action Step: What are some of the things that you have had to "give up" along your spiritual journey? God will often ask us to release things, as a move of faith and wisdom (or He'll just take them away if we're stubborn). However, it is often difficult for us to relinquish things that bring us immediate happiness or comfort. It's important to acknowledge and grieve these things. God may have asked you to give it up, but He understands you are human and will struggle. Grieve. Heal. And then hustle.

Week 30

God's Timing

[1] For everything there is a season, a time for every activity under heaven... [7] A time to tear and a time to mend. A time to be quiet and a time to speak. [8] A time to love and a time to hate. A time for war and a time for peace.

(Ecclesiastes 3:1, 7-8 NIV)

Reflection: Many times, we have good intentions, good ideas, good revelation, but our timing is off. Waiting on God's timing is part of the equation to success. We can't work on our own timeline! This is hard and frustrating, but we must ask for patience. Patience to understand when to speak and when to be quiet, patience to know when to move and when to sit still, patience to move on God's timeline.

Action Step: Working on our patience is probably one of the hardest things that God asks of us. This is particularly more difficult when we are attempting to remain focused and patient while watching God bless others around us, in ways which we prayed for ourselves. Do not be misled. God uses those experiences to work on our hearts and our commitment to Him. What is an area of your life that you lack patience in, that you would like God to heal and help you?

Abigail- Success

Wrap Up

By the standards of many; wealth, beauty and intelligence are considered "success." Abigail must have been considered successful for her assets, but God's definition of success looks different and feels different. While it's easy to get caught up in superficial things like looks and status, God had Abigail caught up in purpose, wealth, breaking generational curses, strengthening her lineage, and establishing HIS kingdom. She was focused. For us to reach God's potential of success for our lives, we must be open to accepting the challenges of success. Abigail saw an opportunity to utilize what God had given her, her gift of prophecy. Seizing this opportunity required her to look at things from the outside in, to gain an unbiased perspective. The opportunity required her to practice humility and ask for forgiveness. Abigail knew the Lord and this allowed her to know what to say and when to say it. Without knowing God she would have fumbled the ball and tried to explain herself away, when that was NOT what the encounter with David or her encounter with opportunity required. Abigail knew when to move, when to activate her gift of prophecy and when to stay quiet. Her dependence on God's timeline ensured that her opportunity made an impact. Opportunities for growth and excellence surround us all the time, but are we willing and capable of taking on the challenge? Or are we content in our corner with our faulty, biased, and mediocre definitions of success? Rising to the challenge of creating success in the Lord's kingdom requires perspective. Things are not always cause and effect when it comes to God. Remaining in constant connection with God is key to changing our perspective and allows for us to recognize opportunities in challenges which will result in success beyond our wildest dreams.

Action Step: God will often use what the world deems as a weakness to demonstrate His strength. What are some of your personal characteristics that one may consider a "weakness?" Please list them below. (We encourage you to simply pray and ask God to make what you consider weaknesses, your strengths. Watch God show up.)

Month 8

Biblical Leader: Naomi

Devotion Topic: Long-suffering IS a blessing

13 So Boaz took Ruth and she became his wife. Then he went to her, and the
Lord enabled her to conceive, and she gave birth to a son. 14 The women said
to Naomi: "Praise the Lord, who this day has not left you without a kinsman-
redeemer. May he become famous throughout Israel! 15 He will renew your life
and sustain you in your old age. For your daughter-in-law, who loves you and
who is better to you than seven sons, has given him birth." 16 Then Naomi took
the child, laid him in her lap and cared for him. 17 The women living there said
"Naomi has a son." And they named him Obed. He was the father of Jesse, who
was the father of David.

(Ruth 4:13-17 NIV)

We previously mentioned Naomi as part of Ruth's story. This month we'll focus on Naomi's personal story, her perspective and how the Lord presented Himself in her life.

Naomi was married to Elimelech and they lived in the promised land (the land that God had promised to his people in exile). There was now famine in the promised land and Naomi, along with her husband and sons, had no choice but to forfeit their land and inheritance, in efforts to move to another town in search of a better life. So, they headed to Moab. While in Moab her sons married Moabite women, despite the law prohibiting marriage with pagan women. Sometime later, Naomi became a widow. Soon after, both of her sons died leaving her destitute with her two daughters-in-law. Having nothing else in Moab, Naomi decided to return to her home in Judah. Naomi attempted to have her daughters-in-law return to their families, as she believed that the Lord's hand had gone out against her (in other words, she felt like God had forgotten her). However, her daughter-in-law, Ruth, refused to leave her side. Once back in her homeland, she was recognized by others and they asked if she was Naomi. She replied, "don't call me Naomi, call me Mara, because the Almighty has made my life very bitter." Naomi explained that she was full when she left Bethlehem and she knew she had returned empty. Naomi encouraged Ruth to collect the barley and go to Boaz, as he was a relative and a kinsman-redeemer (a relative that could reclaim the inheritance of property). Ruth did just that and ended up marrying Boaz. Boaz bought all of Naomi's husband's property to maintain the family name on record. Ruth and Boaz bore a son, Naomi's grandson and continued their lineage. Ultimately, Naomi found joy again in her new life: a new grandson, wealth and stability. But it was not without her sustaining a season of longsuffering.

Month 8

Biblical Leader: Naomi

Devotion Topic: Long-suffering IS a blessing

1.Naomi's longsuffering: Naomi had a long road of suffering. Although she had inherited land, she had to leave because of a famine. Then her sons married pagan women (women that she ended up loving, but that she might not have adored initially). She then lost her husband and subsequently lost her sons. With the loss of the men in her life, she also lost her financial stability, her secured future and any chance at a lineage or inheritance. For Naomi, it was one thing after the next.

2.Naomi's displacement: Naomi was removed from her home, her people, her family and her future. She had nothing but God's promise to Ruth and Ruth's commitment to Naomi and her God.

3.Naomi's embarrassment/brokenness: When Naomi returned to Bethlehem, she was NOT the same woman. She felt this so strongly that she changed her name to Mara. She realized that she left her home and people full; with a husband, a family and a future, and she was now returning empty. She returned old, a widow and with a pagan girl by her side. I'm sure she was filled with feelings of frustration, shame and defeat.

4.Naomi's Redeemer: Naomi was NOT the woman who left Bethlehem, she had been broken, dismantled, and emptied. But God! God swept in and redeemed her. He gave her a family, a home, a grandchild, a lineage, and security. God blessed Naomi more abundantly than she could have imagined. He blessed Naomi to establish His Kingdom and prepare the lineage of Jesus.

Week 31

The purpose of suffering and tribulations

2 My fellow believers, when it seems as though you are facing nothing but
difficulties, see it as an invaluable opportunity to experience the greatest joy
that you can! 3 For you know that when your faith is tested it stirs up power
within you to endure all things. 4 And then as your endurance grows even
stronger it will release perfection into every part of your being until there is
nothing missing and nothing lacking.

(James 1: 2-4 TPT)

Reflection: During periods of long- suffering, God allows us to journey through a range of emotions that can include doubt, fear, confusion and/or depression. We must remember that our current suffering is an investment in our future blessings, blessings that are on the way. The difficult times prepare us for the blessings and the responsibility of being highly blessed and favored.

Action Step: What are some of the trials that you have faced on your journey? Which ones have you conquered and which ones are still a challenge? (Remember, each trial that we survive and conquer, is proof that we can handle all that is to come.)

Week 32

Finding our way after being displaced

[11] He gives prosperity to the poor and protects those who suffer.

(Job 5:11 NLT)

Reflection: God has purpose and intent for us. We simply need to remain faithful and open to His blessings. Whatever was taken from us, wherever we were displaced to, God will provide in abundance. Blessings come in many shapes and forms that aren't always obvious, especially when we've experienced significant hurt in the past. But God promises to bless those who have suffered and have remained faithful.

Action Step: Praise report time! Name one time in your life when God has brought you through. When He has shown up in your life in an unimaginable way? (Hint: If you are having trouble with this one, we encourage you to DIG DEEP. If you are having trouble finding God's hand in your life, then you may also be struggling with demonstrating gratitude for what God has done.) Pay attention to everything. Even the "small" things.

Week 33

What do I do with my shame/embarrassment?

12-13 I know what it means to lack, and I know what it means to experience overwhelming abundance. For I'm trained in the secret of overcoming all things, whether in fullness or in hunger. And I find that the strength of Christ's explosive power infuses me to conquer every difficulty.

(Philippians 4:12-13 TPT)

Reflection: Take perspective... We got this! Why? Because God said so! He already told us that He has our back and will strengthen us to endure whatever we face. So, we don't walk around foolishly thinking we will not encounter any trouble nor that we will be defeated by what has happened to us. We simply walk in strength, holding fast to His promise that all will be well and that we will come out victorious.

Action Step: Long-suffering can show up in our lives in a number of ways and we can only control one aspect of long-suffering, how we respond to it. How do you respond to trials in your life? Are you happy with your crisis response method? (Because that's literally what it is)

Week 34

My Redeemer

[11] The Lord will guide you continually, giving you water when you are dry and restoring your strength. You will be like a well-watered garden, like an ever-flowing spring. [12] Some of you will rebuild the deserted ruins of your cities. Then you will be known as a rebuilder of walls and a restorer of homes.

(Isaiah 58: 11-12 NLT)

Reflection: Suffering teaches us how to remain focused, humble and grateful. We learn how to start implementing the fruits of the Spirit. Do not be discouraged in hard times. Regard it as proof of success to come. Our God will stand with us and have our back. He stands in the gap for us when we cannot stand for ourselves. This suffering can be the key to our legacy, to what God wants to create in us.

Action Step: What are some of the lessons you've learned as a result of suffering or feeling pain? How can you use these lessons to propel your future?

Naomi- Long-suffering IS a blessing

Wrap Up

Naomi suffered for a long time. She suffered so deeply, that she began to believe the Lord had turned against her. She was displaced from all she knew and all she had. To top it off, she had to endure the embarrassment and shame of returning to her home without a thing to show for it (and there wasn't TV in those days so we can only imagine all the gossip at the city gates). She saw herself as having left full and having returned empty. But God was in control. God had a purpose for Naomi's life. What Naomi thought she had was only a small fragment of what God had planned for her. While she rightfully mourned her losses, God was planning to make her the grandmother of David, ancestor to Solomon, and eventually Jesus himself. Many times, we see our own suffering as never-ending. We can't seem to catch a break. However, it is important for us to understand in those times that we are seeing only a small piece of the puzzle and God has the whole puzzle figured out. Many of us have been displaced from our families, our homes, our communities, our dreams, our rightful inheritances, our hopes, etc. It may look like this is the end, like there is no getting it back. We might be right, there might be no "getting it back", God makes no promises of that. But He does promise blessings, protection and a future. He promises things that have not even entered our minds. The shame we might feel from what we lost and what people around us might be thinking can stop us from pursuing God's will in our lives. Even what we think of ourselves can serve as a major roadblock. But God doesn't care about any of that! He has come to redeem us, to re-establish His kingdom. So, all the fretting about what we had and what we lost will seem frivolous when we encounter our Redeemer and see ourselves as the redeemed.

Action Step: Your situation is temporary. Seasons change and the bible tells us, mourning may endure for the night but joy will come in the morning. (Psalm 30:5) Your time is coming. Your situation will change. But while you are here, what do you think God is trying to teach you, in this season?

Month 9

Biblical Leader: Mary of Bethany
Devotion Topic: Gratitude

Six days before the Passover, Jesus arrived at Bethany, where Lazarus lived,
whom Jesus had raised from the dead. [2] Here a dinner was given in Jesus'
honor. Martha served, while Lazarus was among those reclining at the table
with him. [3] Then Mary took about a pint of pure nard, an expensive perfume;
she poured it on Jesus' feet and wiped his feet with her hair. And the house
was filled with the fragrance of the perfume. [4] But one of his disciples, Judas
Iscariot, who was later to betray him, objected, [5] "Why wasn't this perfume
sold and the money given to the poor? It was worth a year's wages." [6] He did
not say this because he cared about the poor but because he was a thief; as
keeper of the money bag, he used to help himself to what was put into it. [7]
"Leave her alone," Jesus replied. "It was intended that she should save this
perfume for the day of my burial. [8] You will always have the poor among you,
but you will not always have me."

(John 12:1-7)

Mary of Bethany was a believer and friend of Jesus. She, along with her brother Lazarus and sister Martha, believed in Jesus and followed His teachings. Lazarus had been sick and Jesus promised that Lazarus would not die because God would use the opportunity for His glory. When Lazarus passed away, Mary grieved until she was summoned by Jesus. She came to Lazarus's tomb and was a witness to her brother's resurrection. After the resurrection, Jesus limited his public appearances because He was being openly persecuted. However, right before Passover, He visited Mary, Martha, and Lazarus for a gathering. While He visited, Lazarus sat and listened to Jesus teach and speak. Martha was busy hosting and making sure everything was prepared for her guests, especially her guest of honor. All the while, Mary sat at the feet of Jesus and listened. She was moved to gather a fragrance, probably her most expensive possession and pour it at the feet of Jesus. She then dried His feet with her own hair. One of the disciples there criticized her, but Jesus came to her defense and acknowledged Mary's gesture as one of gratitude and reverence.

Month 9

Biblical Leader: Mary of Bethany
Devotion Topic: Gratitude

1. Mary was a witness: Mary had witnessed Jesus' teachings. She was part of His circle and had heard what He was doing with His people. Mary also had a personal experience when she was grieving the loss of her brother and Jesus resurrected him. Jesus had told Mary and her sister that Lazarus would be okay and just as He promised, it happened.

2. Mary acknowledged Jesus: When Jesus came to their home, Mary could have tended to her guests and helped host like her sister did. She could have sat back, relaxed and enjoyed the conversation like Lazarus. But instead, Mary recognized there was something special happening in her home. Something that required her to slow down, sit still, and listen. Mary was attuned with Jesus's spirit.

3. Mary gave Him her all: Mary showed her love to Jesus with all she had, her most expensive fragrance. The text is not explicit, but we can guess that she did not just pour a drop, she most likely emptied the bottle on Him. She had no qualms or hesitations about what she was willing to give. She didn't think twice about her sacrifice.

4. Mary's act of gratitude: When Mary was ready to pour her love and demonstrate her gratitude, not only did she give her best, but she also gave of herself. The scripture states that she went on her knees and used her own hair to dry His feet. Mary was so in awe and grateful for what Jesus had done for her, that she did not care what was at stake, who was watching, who had an opinion or how foolish she might have looked.

5. Mary's critics: Let's picture this: Jesus is talking (most likely to a group of men), He is surrounded by His disciples and here is Mary at His feet pouring a fragrance and wiping His feet with her hair. Of course, someone had something to say! A man had something to say to embarrass her and to minimize her offering. But Jesus saw right through that. He saw her heart and her intention. He immediately defended her and her actions.

Week 35

Being a witness

[14] "Look, the highest heavens and the earth and everything in it all belong to the Lord your God. [15] Yet the Lord chose your ancestors as the objects of his love. And he chose you, their descendants, above all other nations, as is evident today. [16] Therefore, change your hearts and stop being stubborn. [17] "For the Lord your God is the God of gods and Lord of lords. He is the great God, the mighty and awesome God, who shows no partiality and cannot be bribed... [21] He alone is your God, the only one who is worthy of your praise, the one who has done these mighty miracles that you have seen with your own eyes.

(Deuteronomy 10:14-17, 21 NLT)

Reflection: He is the King of kings! The Lord of lords! He is great! He is mighty! The ONLY one worthy of our praise! He has and will continue to do miracles beyond our wildest imaginations. We worship Him because of who He is!

Action Step: God simply wants us to praise Him. It's literally that simple. As you read this and in this exact moment, we would like you to take a deep breath and thank God. Simply for who HE is. Use the space below to freely write out your praises unto Him.

Week 36

Acknowledging all that we have been given

[17] Let every activity of your lives and every word that comes from your lips be drenched with the beauty of our Lord Jesus, the Anointed One. And bring your constant praise to God the Father because of what Christ has done for you!

(Colossians 3:17 TPT)

Reflection: We are already equipped for the journey. He has given us exactly what we need to start. We are prepared. We step out into the world filled with love, cloaked in strength and prepared for the journey ahead. Acknowledge His work in our lives and in the lives of others. Do not turn a blind eye to where He has taken us from. Acknowledge and praise Him for what He has done!

Action Step: What sets you apart? God gives us all our own little quirks, passions and skill sets. All these characteristics somehow play into His larger plan. What has God equipped you with (e.g., a keen sense of humor, great organizational skills, public speaking comfortability, etc.)?

Week 37

Giving Him our ALL

[9] May my satisfaction be found in you. Don't let me be so rich that I don't need you or so poor that I have to resort to dishonesty just to make ends meet. Then my life will never detract from bringing glory to your name.

(Proverbs 30:9 TPT)

Reflection: We often focus on what we have or don't have, but when we realize that it all comes from HIM and that He satisfies all of our needs, it is easy to give Him our all. After all, how could we not give Him our best, when He gave us our best?

Action Step: Are you giving God the best version of you? Or better yet, are you showing up in this world as the best version of yourself? If not, what can you do to show up in your life in all of God's glory?

Week 38

How do we demonstrate gratitude?

[16] Let joy be your continual feast. [17] Make your life a prayer. [18] God's perfect plan for you in Christ Jesus.

(1 Thessalonians 5:16-18 TPT)

Reflection: Praise Him, at all times and in all things. Make your praise loud, flamboyant, ridiculous and worthy of Him. This is how we show gratitude. We show Him our gratitude for what He has done, what He is doing and what He will do through praise and worship. In the midst of everything we need to continually give thanks, for this is what God wants. He wants us to be content and show gratitude in all situations, at all times.

Action Step: The thought of remaining in a place of contentment and gratitude can be difficult. It is most difficult when we are feeling frustrated, alone and overwhelmed. But, even in those situations we have SOMETHING to be grateful for. In your darkest hour, what do you have to be grateful for?

Week 39

Remaining focused on God's will

57 ...then Jesus told them, "A prophet is honored everywhere except in his own hometown and among his own family."

(Matthew 13:57 NLT)

Reflection: People will hate. People will try to discredit you, take your shine, ridicule you, and shame you. Prepare for it. Process it. And keep it moving. Let God fight those battles. Do not become so distracted by it that it keeps you from your purpose or praise and worship. God needs us to remain focused on Him, so that we may fulfill His purpose for us on earth.

Action Step: We could focus on how hurtful the things people say about us are, but instead, in true Bawse fashion we want to focus on who WE are. So, what are some of the LIES people have said about who you are? What do you plan to do to live your life in a way that defies (or ignores) those assumptions?

Mary of Bethany- Gratitude

Wrap Up

Mary of Bethany had seen Jesus's works and had personally experienced Jesus resurrecting her emotions from a place of grief to a place of joy. She carried herself like a witness of Jesus's deeds. Mary acknowledged Jesus's presence in her life. She acknowledged what He had done for her. She lived her life attuned to God and sought out opportunities to display her gratitude to Jesus. When Mary decided to honor Jesus, she gave her all. She displayed her gratitude with all she had and all of who she was. When the haters spoke up, Mary kept quiet and let Jesus fight her battles. We have been witnesses, one way or another, to what God has done in our lives or in the lives of others. We have seen how God flips something that is meant to hurt us into something that will propel us to the next level. Let us walk around this world bearing witness to the works of our God. Let us acknowledge what He has done for us, that there might not be a doubt in others' minds that everything we are and have comes from our Redeemer. Let us live our life in a way that says we give our all to God, because He has given us His all. We will be grateful at all times for His works in our lives. We will show our unapologetic gratitude to God, despite what others may think or say.

Action Step: Mary simply didn't care. She lived BOLDLY. She felt no need to live by the standards others placed before her, as long as she was pleasing Christ. The audacity of this woman, to chuck the deuces in the air and march to the beat of her own drum! There is liberation in her bold demeanor. What is your demeanor? Are you living BOLDLY in your truth and passion? If not, that's holding you back. What do you need to do to remove that roadblock?

Month 10

Biblical Leader: Rahab
Devotion Topic: Leading Others

[8] Before the spies lay down for the night, she went up on the roof [9] and said to them, "I know that the Lord has given this land to you and that a great fear of you has fallen on us, so that all who live in this country are melting in fear because of you. [10] We have heard how the Lord dried up the water of the Red Sea for you when you came out of Egypt, and what you did to Sihon and Og, the two kings of the Amorites east of the Jordan, whom you completely destroyed. [11] When we heard of it, our hearts melted and everyone's courage failed because of you, for the Lord your God is God in heaven above and on the earth below. [12] Now then, please swear to me by the Lord that you will show kindness to my family, because I have shown kindness to you. Give a sure sign [13] that you will spare the lives of my father and mother, my brothers and sisters, and all who belong to them, and that you will save us from death." [14] "Our lives for your lives!" the men assured her. "If you don't tell what we are doing, we will treat you kindly and faithfully when the Lord gives us the land."

(Joshua 2:8-14 NIV)

Rahab was a prostitute who lived inside the heavily fortressed wall of Jericho. Jericho was part of the land that God had promised His people after He led them out of Egypt and it would be their first battle into the promised land. God's people had witnessed many miracles in their travels from Egypt to the promised land. The news of those miracles had traveled and reached many places, including Jericho. The people of Jericho had heard of what God had done for His people and were afraid. The king of Jericho learned that Joshua (the leader of God's people) had sent spies to his land, so the king sent messengers to Rahab who asked her to bring out the men who had entered her home. Unbeknownst to them, Rahab had hidden the two men on her roof. When the king's messengers came, she told them the men had left. Rahab then went up to the roof and told the spies that she knew the Lord had given them the land of Jericho and that the people of Jericho were fearful of them. She admitted that she had heard of the miracles that God had given His people and how those miracles had instilled fear in her people. Rahab also recognized that their God was the God of Heaven and Earth. She asked them to spare her and her family because of the kindness she had shown them (Rahab was savvy). The spies agreed to spare her and her family from destruction when they returned, if she kept their hiding place secret. The spies then returned to Joshua and told him what had transpired. Later, when Joshua gave the orders to enter and take hold of the promised land, he instructed his men to destroy every living thing except for Rahab and the people in her home. When the entire city was burned, Rahab and her family were taken outside the camp of Israel where they lived among the Israelites. Rahab changed her life. She got married, settled down and ultimately became the mother of Boaz, kinsman-redeemer of Ruth and Naomi, lineage of King David, King Solomon, and eventually Jesus himself.

Month 10

Biblical Leader: Rahab
Devotion Topic: Leading Others

1. Rahab was a sinner: The scriptures state that Rahab was a prostitute, a woman who provided sexual favors for compensation. I'm sure during those days, people probably looked down on her, talked trash about her, and most definitely counted her out. Prostitution is a profession that sits in the underbelly of most societies. People who engage in this form of labor are thought to be inadequate, "illegal", of low moral character and undeserving of empathy and support. This was how Rahab was viewed in her society. No one expects a leader to grow from the underbelly of society... but God!

2. Rahab knew the "tea": The thing with Rahab was, even though she was at the margins of her society, she had heard some things (probably because the streets be talking, but that's a story for another day). Rahab had heard what God had done for the Israelites. She had heard about how God had liberated them from Egypt and how He provided miracles along the way. Even though she was NOT a part of the elite or the "chosen", she had heard the stories and she was paying attention.

3. Rahab took a position: When the spies came to Rahab's home, she hid them. And when the king's messengers came to inquire, she protected them. Rahab took a position. She stood in the gap. Instead of following orders, she decided to lead her life and the lives of her loved ones in the direction of the Lord, the God she had heard of. She could have surrendered the spies and maybe gained some notoriety and respect from the king and his people. However, Rahab had heard of the Lord. She had heard how powerful and transformative He could be in her life. She was not certain, but she took a position and put it all on the line. What she stood to gain was greater than what she stood to lose and Rahab knew that. That's what leaders do. We don't always know the outcome; we simply have to trust God to bless us with good judgement and the ability to demonstrate it in high stress situations.

4. Rahab led her family: Rahab was a savvy leader, a hustler to say the least. When Rahab interceded for her life, she also interceded for the lives of her family members. She takes the position of leading her unknowing family into a way of life that centered around the grace of God. It's likely she was not the most respected member of that family due to the way she made a living. Yet, that did not stop her from taking a position and leading her family to the truth. She chose to step up, be a leader and protect her family at all costs. In spite of her harsh beginning, she, Rahab, the prostitute, became the family's redeemer (Interestingly, this is how her son, Boaz, is also later described in the bible.) Rahab left a legacy.

Week 40

We are all sinners...

22 This righteousness is given through faith in Jesus Christ to all who believe.
There is no difference between Jew and Gentile, 23 for all have sinned and fall
short of the glory of God, 24 and all are justified freely by his grace through the
redemption that came by Christ Jesus.

(Romans 3:23-24)

Reflection: We have ALL sinned. It doesn't matter if you are a Jew or Gentile, heathen or atheist, goody-two shoes or sketchy, put together or a hot mess, we have ALL sinned and come up short. The only one that can justify us and redeem us, is God.

Action Step: The bible consistently reminds us to enter God's presence with a clean and pure heart. This means openly admitting our shortcomings to God and asking Him to heal us in these areas. Please understand God is all knowing and thus He already knows your mistakes. He simply wants us to demonstrate humility and trust in Him. What do you need to admit to God today, before you can enter His presence with a pure heart? What will you ask God for forgiveness for today? (You can use the space below to jot down your thoughts or not. No need to write it down if you choose not to. Simply open your mouth and speak the words aloud for God to hear.)

Week 41

We are all sinners...

[17] Consequently, faith comes from hearing the message, and the message is heard through the word about Christ.

(Romans 10:17 NIV)

Reflection: All we have to do is hear the message, hear of the miracles, hear of the transformations that God has accomplished in those around us. That is how we increase our faith. We are exposed to the wonders of God by hearing. However, in order to HEAR of God's goodness, those who are redeemed must be willing to SPEAK and ANNOUNCE the goodness of our Lord.

Action Step: What has God done for you? What testimonies are you shouting from the rooftops? We challenge you to pick three things God has done for you in your life and list them below. Now, take a moment to truly, whole-heartedly thank God for showing up for you in those ways and then ask Him to continue to show up for you in this manner moving forward.

Week 42

Positioning yourself to lead others

9 This is my command—be strong and courageous! Do not be afraid or discouraged. For the Lord your God is with you wherever you go.

(Joshua 1:9 NLT)

Reflection: We lead by example. Fear not, for God is with us. Rahab must have felt afraid when the king's messengers were at her door. She must have also experienced fear when the spies arrived and she decided to negotiate with them. However, this did not stop Rahab. She had a need, a need to know more about the God of miracles. And when everyone around her moved in fear, she moved in faith. She moved in the faith, which had grown in her, through what she had heard of God.

Action Step: As leaders, we lead exactly how we show up in life. If we are timid and fearful, that is how we tend to lead. If we are brave and savvy, that is how we show up in this world. Rahab's past, which trained her to be bold and savvy, gave her the exact skills she needed to show up as a Godly leader in this world (though the skill was learned through ungodly methods). How are you showing up as a leader (of your family, job, church, social group, etc.) and how did you learn/foster these skills? (Please note: Both positive and negative characteristics should be included and processed. If it isn't healthy, drop the behavior. If it is healthy, increase it.)

Week 43

Leading in your personal life, first.

[2] "Enlarge your house; build an addition. Spread out your home and spare no expense! [3] For you will soon be bursting at the seams. Your descendants will occupy other nations and resettle the ruined cities.

(Isaiah 54:2-3 NLT)

Reflection: God is telling us that He is about to enlarge our territory. He is promising to make us a part of His legacy. How could we not be grateful? How could we be so selfish to think that we accomplish all this on our own? God is prepared to do HUGE things in our lives and our families have front row seats to what the Lord is doing. Get ready! Praise Him now! Praise Him in advance!

Action Step: How are you preparing for the huge testimony about to unfold in your life? (e.g., Are you establishing a routine that supports more blessings and responsibilities? Are you saving money to invest in the purpose God has laid before you? Are you teaching your children humility, before the blessing? How are you making room for the blessings that are on the way?)

Rahab- Leading Others

Wrap Up

Rahab was a prostitute, discredited, probably even unwanted, but God considered her NECESSARY for His kingdom. Rahab had heard of what God was doing with His people and hearing was enough for her. Hearing was enough to increase her faith and propel her to take a stance. Her hearing and faith lead her family and the people of God to the promised land to fulfill God's promises. Without her, the word of promise that God had given His people many years ago, would not have come to fruition. Without Rahab, there would be no Solomon and David. Rahab, who the world might have thought was insignificant, was essential to God's promise and kingdom. God does not care that you are a sinner, He does not care about what you have done, how respected you are, whether you are worthy or not, who likes you or who doesn't. All He cares about is that you hear and have faith. That your faith moves you to take a position that only you (with your faults and virtues) can take to lead His people unto Him.

Action Step: We have all felt unwanted, discredited and under-appreciated at times. But Rahab didn't let any of those feelings impede on her purpose. She stayed focused on her goal of protecting her family, despite her feelings. Though she felt fearful, she showed up cloaked in bravery. What negative feeling are you willing to replace with an even stronger action? (e.g., I am giving up my need for perfection and showing up determined to only walk in purpose, even if it isn't perfect. What's yours?)

Action Step: I can only assume that Rahab wanted to be more than simply a prostitute. So, she waited until God provided another avenue, then seized the opportunity and never looked back. Often, we are so overwhelmed with our own hustle and views of success that we aren't even aware of God's opportunities. We are too focused on our own goals. This isn't a question that requires a written answer. Simply a thought-provoking question for you: Are you paying attention? Would you KNOW if God sent the right opportunity? If not, we encourage you to start praying for clarity and focus when in the presence of the Lord.

Month 11

Biblical Leader: Leah
Devotion Topic: Coping with Success

[31] When the Lord saw that Leah was not loved, he opened her womb, but Rachel
was barren. [32] Leah became pregnant and gave birth to a son. She named him
Reuben, for she said, "It is because the Lord has seen my misery. Surely my
husband will love me now." [33] She conceived again, and when she gave birth to
a son she said, "Because the Lord heard that I am not loved, he gave me this
one too." So she named him Simeon. [34] Again she conceived, and when she
gave birth to a son she said, "Now at last my husband will become attached
to me, because I have borne him three sons." So he was named Levi. [35] She
conceived again, and when she gave birth to a son she said, "This time I will
praise the Lord." So she named him Judah. Then she stopped having children.

(Genesis 29:31-35 NIV)

Leah was Rachel's older sister. They were daughters of Laban. The bible says that Leah "had weak eyes, but Rachel was lovely in form, and beautiful". Jacob showed up, saw Rachel, fell in love with her and offered to work for her father for seven years in exchange for Rachel's hand in marriage. Laban agreed and Jacob worked for seven years. When the time came, Jacob asked for his wife, but instead of Rachel, he got Leah. When Jacob asked about the switch, Laban told him that it was tradition for the oldest daughter to marry first. Laban agreed to also give him Rachel if he would commit to another seven years of work. Jacob once again agreed and Rachel became his wife. Leah felt the rejection and lack of love from her husband Jacob. She knew he loved Rachel. Yet, God saw that Leah was not loved and allowed her to have many children. Every time Leah bore a son, she thought she was closer to getting what she wanted, Jacob's love. However, as she continued to conceive she came to realize that God had not given her Jacob's love, but He had given her other gifts, her children. All the while, Rachel was barren. While Leah was jealous of Rachel for the love she had from Jacob, Rachel was jealous of the blessings (children) Leah received. Eventually, Leah conceived six sons and a daughter, including Levi (which led to the priestly lineage) and Judah (which led to the tribe of Judah, lineage of King David, King Solomon, and eventually the Messiah himself, Jesus).

Month 11

Biblical Leader: Leah
Devotion Topic: Coping with Success

1. Leah's self-esteem: Leah's self-esteem must have been at a low point. The bible notes that she was not as beautiful as her sister and on top of that, the man she married loved her sister and not her. The way she saw herself must have been shaped by her circumstances and how she was treated by those around her.

2. Leah did not get what she wanted: Leah wanted one thing, Jacob's love, but no matter how hard she tried or how many sons she bore him she could not seem to have that.

3. Leah's impact on others: As Leah was consumed by what she thought about herself and what she did NOT have, she had little awareness that she did have something her sister wanted. Leah had been blessed with children and Rachel was barren. So, while Leah was jealous of Jacob's love for Rachel, Rachel was jealous of Leah's blessing, her ability to bear children.

4. Leah's process: Leah started off attempting to get what she wanted through her blessings. This process can be observed when we look at where her head is at after every birth. After each son was born:

1. The Lord has seen my misery
2. Because the Lord heard that I am not loved

3. Now my husband will become attached to me because I have borne him three sons
4. This time I will praise the Lord
5. God has rewarded me
6. God has presented me with a precious gift, this time my husband will treat me with honor

5.Leah's success: Leah started off wanting Jacob's love, but God decided to bless her with children instead. Leah attempted to use her blessings to get what she wanted, but that was not God's intention. Instead, after every birth, Leah gained a better understanding of her gifts and she began to understand the purpose of her gifts. What started as Leah noting her misery, ended with her acknowledgment that God had presented her with a precious gift.

Week 44

My Self-Esteem

[13] You formed my innermost being, shaping my delicate inside and my intricate outside, and wove them all together in my mother's womb. [14] I thank you, God, for making me so mysteriously complex! Everything you do is marvelously breathtaking. It simply amazes me to think about it! How thoroughly you know me, Lord!

(Psalm 139:13-14 TPT)

Reflection: We must learn to see ourselves in God's image. He created each one of us to be unique and wondrous. He doesn't expect us to conform, but rather, transform. Stand in your power and in your truth. You were literally made for this.

Action Step: To experience the true heights of success we must live up to all that God intended for us to be, but we often limit ourselves due to our own misconceptions. In one sentence describe yourself.

Now write one sentence on how you believe God would describe you. (If there is a discrepancy between the two, understand your description is wrong and work needs to be done to start walking in the path God has laid out for you.)

Week 45

Not getting what I prayed for

[28] And we know that in all things God works for the good of those who love him, who have been called according to his purpose.

(Romans 8:28 NIV)

Reflection: God promises to work out everything for your good. He doesn't promise to give you everything you want! Sometimes we are so caught up in what we want and what we can't have, that we miss the blessings, gifts and opportunities that we do have. If we stop getting caught up in what we want and let God give us what He has worked out for us, we will be more than happy. We will experience joy in God's purpose.

Action Step: The hardest part about living in #PurposeNProfits is that God controls our destiny, not us. He knows the desires of our heart and sees our sacrifice, but His will and His Kingdom are the ultimate priority. God blesses us in unimaginable ways if we are willing to follow His path. What has God led you to do that you don't want to do or that leads you away from your idea of success? Are you willing to trust God in this area even if it means you are not moving closer to YOUR idea of success?

Week 46

How others see me

[29] If you are uniquely gifted in your work, you will rise and be promoted. You won't be held back—you'll stand before kings!

(Proverbs 22:29 TPT)

Reflection: It doesn't matter. As long as we show up and handle business, we will be well. Others will have their opinions, their feelings and their judgements; but when we focus on God and our gift, none of that matters.

Action Step: People think a whole lot about a whole lot of nothing. With that said, how people think of us or the judgements they might pass, is of no concern or consequence to the authors of this book. We simply focus on how WE will show up in this world. So, bump what anyone else thinks. How do YOU want to be seen in this world? What will your legacy be?

Week 47

The process of success

[10] Those who love money will never have enough. How meaningless to think that wealth brings true happiness! [11] The more you have, the more people come to help you spend it. So what good is wealth—except perhaps to watch it slip through your fingers!

(Ecclesiastes 5:10-11 NLT)

Reflection: We often equate success with financial wealth. While this can be true for some, financial wealth can be daunting and detrimental for others. Walking into our purpose in God's kingdom is a process. During the process we learn what God wants us to be and to let go of what we want. Be mindful of your heart, your intentions and your obedience to God's will. We have all heard the saying; "If I knew then, what I know now...".

Action Step: Will it all be worth it? If you were to get everything you ever hoped for, but the journey was absolutely horrible, would it have been worth it? Ask yourself this early on. (Oftentimes, we think we know what we want until we experience what we must go through to get it. Consider your dreams and truly ask yourself, 'If I lose it all going after this dream, is it worth it?')

Week 48

What is the purpose of my success?

[3] Be free from pride-filled opinions, for they will only harm your cherished unity. Don't allow self-promotion to hide in your hearts, but in authentic humility put others first and view others as more important than yourselves.

(Philippians 2:3 TPT)

Reflection: Love God's people. Care for them and live in purpose. As we share His Agape love, the world is healed little by little, allowing others to stand in their purpose. The purpose of our success is to make us witnesses of God's power for others.

Action Step: Godly wisdom teaches us that our own achievements can only be considered true successes if we fulfill our purpose in God's Kingdom. As humans, we can experience a bunch of other kinds of success, but for Christians this is it. Do your dreams and goals fall in line with your purpose? If not, how can they become aligned?

Leah- Coping with Success

Wrap Up

In any traditional story, Leah would have been the character that we all pitied. However, in God's story, Leah is the character that grows and transforms into something bigger than herself.

Leah's self-esteem was shattered because she didn't have the love of her husband (I think we can all empathize with not having love reciprocated in one way or another, it's the most awful feeling!). Leah was not able to see anything beyond getting what she wanted. She was jealous of her sister, meanwhile God was blessing her left and right. She was so caught up in getting what she wanted that she couldn't see the blessings and favor God was giving her. While she was worried about what was going on with Jacob and Rachel, Leah couldn't see the jealousy that her own sister harbored towards her. It took a process, a God-driven process, to allow Leah to transform her perspective and her thinking from a place of misery to a place of honor.

Leah's success came from God's blessing, but her ability to see her blessing came from the transformation of her thinking. Many of us have been dealt a lousy card in life. But that's our perspective; God sees it differently. God can't wait to take that mess and make it into something beautiful, just so he can let everybody else see how powerful and mighty He is. If we take a minute to step back and stop being so caught up in what we want and think we need, we can see what God is trying to do with us. Whatever it is you think you want will be less than half of what God wants to give you. We get so caught up in what other people have and how other people's lives seem to be going that we miss what God is trying to do in us, in our lives and in our homes. Success in God's purpose is a process. It can be painful, uncomfortable, annoying, exhausting, etc.

Leah had to carry and give birth to six babies to get a glimpse of her position and purpose. It won't happen overnight, but if we say 'yes' to God and His word, then He will carry us through. When we understand that the purpose of our success is not to glorify or exalt and enrich ourselves, but to lead others and to model and personify God's love and promise for others, we step onto a whole new level. A level where our success is not based on how much money we have, how many properties we own or what our portfolio holds. A level where success depends on how much of God we need.

Action Step: Obtaining true success as a Christian woman means committing to live in God's will, even when His will does not align with our desire. Depending on our stage of growth and healing, it might be difficult to see God's hand, especially if we are experiencing deep pain. Take a moment to reflect, then jot down instances that you can recall God blessing you, even when it didn't feel like a blessing. (Remember: Making an effort to remember God's grace in our life opens up the opportunity for God to bless us more. If we do well with a little, God will bless us much more.)

Action Step: Have you ever felt frustrated, jealous or exasperated watching other people live the life you had imagined for yourself? We implore you to think of three people that you believe "have it made" and then see if you can really dig into their stories. Whether you research them online or ask them directly, attempt to see the full picture of their journey. More often than not, you will see that they suffer and struggle just as much and sometimes even more, than we do. They simply choose to keep going. List three people that you will commit to learning more about, including their full story and how they overcame their hurdles.

Month 12

Biblical Leader: The Queen of Sheba
Devotion Topic: Setting the Table

1 When the queen of Sheba heard of Solomon's fame, she came to Jerusalem
to test him with hard questions. Arriving with a very great caravan - with
camels carrying spices, large quantities of gold, and precious stones - she
came to Solomon and talked with him about all she had on her mind. 2 Solomon
answered all her questions; nothing was too hard for him to explain to her. 3
When the queen of Sheba saw the wisdom of Solomon, as well as the palace
he had built, 4 the food on his table, the seating of his officials, the attending
servants in their robes, the cupbearers in their robes and the burnt offerings
he made at the temple of the Lord, she was overwhelmed. 5 She said to the
king, "The report I heard in my own country about your achievements and
your wisdom is true, 6 But I did not believe what they said until I came and saw
with my own eyes. Indeed, not even half the greatness of your wisdom was
told to me; you have far exceeded the report I heard. 7 How happy your men
must be! How happy your officials, who continually stand before you and hear
your wisdom! 8 Praise be to the Lord your God, who has delighted in you and
placed you on his throne as king to rule for the Lord your God. Because of the
love of your God for Israel and his desire to uphold them forever, he has made
you king over them, to maintain justice and righteousness." 9 Then she gave
the king 120 talents of gold, large quantities of spices, and precious stones.
There had never been such spices as those the queen of Sheba gave to King

Solomon. 10 (The men of Hiram and the men of Solomon brought gold from
Ophir; they also brought algumwood and precious stones. 11 The king used the
algumwood to make steps for the temple of the Lord and for the royal palace,
and to make harps and lyres for the musicians. Nothing like them had ever
been seen in Judah.) 12 King Solomon gave the queen of Sheba all she desired
and asked for; he gave her more than she had brought to him. Then she left
and returned with her retinue to her own country.

(2 Chronicles 9:1-12 NIV)

Month 12

Biblical Leader: The Queen of Sheba

Devotion Topic: Setting the Table

The Queen of Sheba was a wealthy ruler of her own prosperous nation. She had heard of the things that God was doing with Solomon and she decided to embark on the long journey to see for herself. She brought him expensive gifts and asked Solomon hard questions, which he was able to answer. She talked to him about what she had on her mind. She realized that the stories of Solomon's wisdom and wealth did not do justice to the realities she was seeing with her eyes. She acknowledged God's role in Solomon's success and praised God. Solomon gave her everything she asked for and more, then she returned to her home. The queen valued wisdom and God honored her with a place in His scriptures. To sum it up, this was a BADDDD Chick. She literally rolled up on Solomon, spent some time being intrigued with his wisdom and knowledge, thanked him for his time, paid him for his troubles and rode back home like it was nobody's business. I often daydream about this queen. Riding through the desert, rich and without a care in the world, but searching for Godly wisdom, despite all that she had.

1. The Queen of Sheba was established: The Queen of Sheba was wealthy and successful in the eyes of most people and according to social standards. She was the ruler of a powerful nation, pretty much a BAWSE. She could move on her own terms. She certainly did not need Solomon, but she wanted to understand.

2. The Queen of Sheba went to meet Solomon herself: With everything that the Queen of Sheba had, she did NOT have to go all the way to Solomon to inquire. She could have sent someone else or been satisfied with the stories she heard. Yet, the queen, with all her power and wealth, decided to go on the long trip herself to see what was going on with Solomon and his God.

3. The Queen of Sheba valued God's wisdom: The Queen of Sheba valued wisdom. When she sought Solomon and checked him out, she quickly realized that this is not of Solomon. She discerned that the wisdom, beauty, and peace that surrounded Solomon came from God. Everything Solomon had came from God's love for him.

4. The Queen of Sheba was in awe: The queen was in awe of what she saw with her eyes and heard with her ears. There was no other explanation, the one responsible for this was God.

Week 49

Getting Established

[3] You have seen everything the Lord your God has done for you during my lifetime. The Lord your God has fought for you against your enemies.

(Joshua 23:3 NLT)

Reflection: If you have made it to this point... you're established! If you are alive and breathing today, God has a purpose for you. God has fought for you and separated you for His kingdom. You are established in God's purpose. He has set the table before you and he has given you what you need to do what He has called you to do.

Action Step: Your promise is your own. Your calling is your own. Your purpose is only meant to fill YOUR soul. What is God calling you to do? Or to put it differently, what do you feel in your heart and tummy, might be your purpose? Start there. God will guide you.

Week 50

My Responsibility

[48]... From everyone who has been given much, much will be demanded; and from the one who has been entrusted with much, much more will be asked.

(Luke 12:48 NIV)

Reflection: If God has given you a purpose and gift, He has blessed you immensely. However, with that blessing, with that success, with that calling, comes great responsibility. You can't just hand this off to an assistant or a junior associate. You have got to do the work. Because at the end of the day God gave this to you, to care for and nurture. He will hold YOU accountable for what you have done with your gifts. Once the table is set, you will be a source of blessing for many and many will be blessed from what you have. But when the rolls run out and the drinks are low, this is your table to tend to.

Action Step: You will have to do it yourself, in the beginning. God spends a lot of time training and molding us to live and thrive in His purpose. When you are just starting out, this will seem extremely overwhelming. But this is YOUR promise. YOUR legacy. YOUR purpose. So yes, you will have to get your hands dirty. The question is, are you ready to live in purpose understanding that it isn't always good times, but that God is with us always? Are you ready to lean into your Godly purpose? If not, what's holding you back?

Week 51

Wisdom above all

[8] "For my thoughts are not your thoughts, neither are your ways my ways," declares the Lord. [9] "As the heavens are higher than the earth, so are my ways higher than your ways and my thoughts than your thoughts.

(Isaiah 55:8-9 NIV)

Reflection: As we walk in our success and the success that God has allowed us to enjoy it is important to seek Him and His wisdom at all times. Just because you think you made it, because your car note is paid for and you can buy designer purses and shoes, does NOT mean you can do this on your own. Look around. EVERYTHING we have came from above. And in all that we do we must consult the BIG man, because our wisdom comes from Him.

Action Step: Obtaining Godly wisdom isn't simply a gift. It takes practice. The more time we spend with a pure heart in the presence of God, the more He makes His path clear to us. It's important to understand that HE places the thoughts of wisdom and discernment in our minds. We can't make it up. His thoughts are not our thoughts! Please list a time when you felt you had to make a decision that you knew God was pushing you to make, but the decision simply didn't make sense? (Please note: God does that a lot. His will, His way often doesn't make sense to us. Doesn't matter. He simply requires our obedience.)

Week 52

In Constant awe of God

5 Trust in the Lord with all your heart and lean not on your own understanding;
6 in all your ways submit to him, and he will make your paths straight. 7 Do
not be wise in your own eyes; fear the Lord and shun evil. 8 This will bring
health to your body and nourishment to your bones. 9 Honor the Lord with your
wealth, with the first fruits of all your crops; 10 then your barns will be filled to
overflowing, and your vats will brim over with new wine.

(Proverbs 3:5-10 NIV)

Reflection: We must constantly be in awe of God's wisdom, love, blessings and care for us. The only way we demonstrate how grateful and devoted we are is by honoring Him in all we do.

Action Step: How will you honor God this week? (e.g., reviewing my gratitude list daily, calling three friends to pray for them, volunteering at a church, screaming His glory from the highest mountain you can find... you get the picture!)

Queen of Sheba- Setting the Table

Wrap Up

The Queen of Sheba was established in her own right, but she recognized that there was more out there. She understood that Solomon's God was more than anything she had or knew. She decided to travel to find out what was going on. She was not too proud to believe the journey to meet Solomon and his God was below her. When she saw and heard the wonders that God had provided Solomon, even though she was a foreigner, she immediately recognized that God was the power behind Solomon's wisdom. She stood in awe of what God had done for Solomon, as it was like nothing she had witnessed before. God has set a table before us. He is offering us His love, compassion, purpose and backing. It is up to us to accept His invitation. He has chosen YOU for this. Only you are equipped to handle this job. Right now, you might not see it in yourself, but when you accept the invite and seek the Lord and His wisdom the picture will be clear and you will be in awe of how God can transform you!

What do you want to learn more about? Like the Queen of Sheba, we leaders must stay learning and stay learning from a Godly perspective. What do you want to learn more about? How can you learn more on this subject and become THE expert?

God has chosen YOU. No more, no less.
Will you choose to show up for Him and live the life HE has chosen for you?

Thank you!

We, strong women led by God, wholly acknowledge the role of the men in our lives in achieving God's purpose. We have a passion for empowering and building up female leaders, however, men also have a role in God's kingdom. Sometimes that role is at the forefront, but sometimes that role is supporting a godly woman from behind the scenes. We thank our brother, Lionel Rodriguez for his contribution of spiritual references and editing to our work. Also, behind the manifestation of this devotional (and our lifestyle) is the relentless support of our husband and life-partner, DeShawn Washington & Keenon Moss. Thank you for having our backs and being top-caliber fathers. Your support enables us to focus on our spirit-filled business. We are forever grateful to our fathers, Noel Rodriguez and the late Carlos Tait, who taught us what to expect from the men in our lives. It goes without saying that we honor our mothers dearly. Their unwavering faith, provision of a solid foundation and fervent prayers have covered us in everything we've accomplished.

A sincere and heartfelt Thank You!
-Dr. Lilliam Rodriguez-Washington & Tiffany Tait, LCSW, CDWF

About the Authors

LILLIAM RODRIGUEZ, PH.D

Dr. Lilliam Rodriguez is a licensed psychologist with over 12 years of experience as a clinical practitioner, behavioral healthcare executive and public speaker. Dr. Rodriguez's unique experience and balanced expertise of optimal clinical care and executive leadership led to her building a successful healthcare consulting firm and medical billing company. After over a decade of successfully juggling the roles of a fulltime mother, wife, executive and entrepreneur, Dr. Rodriguez now resides in the New York City area and provides private executive coaching and behavioral healthcare consulting services. Dr. Rodriguez is fluent in both Spanish and English.

TIFFANY TAIT LCSW, CDWF

Tiffany Tait is a Certified Daring Way facilitator & Licensed Clinical Social Worker (LCSW) who has served the behavioral health community field for over 15 years as a therapist, clinical supervisor, and behavioral healthcare executive. Her multiple roles and distinctive background have led to her expertise in treating clients of diverse backgrounds. Tiffany is most notably recognized for her successes in healthcare program development, executive leadership development, and organizational restructuring. After successfully building seven profitable, multi-million-dollar companies, Tiffany retired from the C-Level suite, and embarked on a new journey of private equity investment. Tiffany currently resides in Florida and spends her time embracing motherhood, coaching, praising God and actively serving on two non-profit organization boards.

Made in the USA
Middletown, DE
04 November 2023